Praise for
Driving Outcomes

"In *Driving Outcomes*, Sarah Plantenberg distills her extensive experience driving innovation into a practical and repeatable methodology that can benefit any business. Having worked closely with Sarah, I saw firsthand how she led enterprises and startups through strategic transformations, turning complex challenges into actionable outcomes. Her book walks readers through a step-by-step framework, including tools designed to help organizations identify goals, enhance collaboration, and drive real business impact."

STEVE ROBINSON, former general manager at IBM Software and senior advisor at IBM and McKinsey

"Bringing one's full self to work is a notion we must be conscious of when understanding how to form culture and define values wherever we are trying to drive outcomes. Sarah Plantenberg gives us permission to do so and to reinforce this when collaborating with others."

ESTHER KIM, global cross brand offering leader at IBM Corporation

"Sarah Plantenberg identifies the 'invisible maze' that humans work through as they try to reconcile their place in a complex workplace culture. Recognizing that this maze exists is the first step in creating a culture that respects and values the humans who comprise it, resulting in an environment where everyone can do their best work."

JASON FRASER, transformation strategy consultant and co-author of *Farther, Faster, and Far Less Drama*

"In *Driving Outcomes*, Sarah Plantenberg deftly illuminates the intricate and often underappreciated connection between organizational culture and business success. This book simplifies complex topics, providing business leaders with practical ways to quickly ignite change."

KIM HEWITT, former IBM sales and consulting executive

"Sarah Plantenberg's *Driving Outcomes* provides a blueprint for how to create the culture your business needs. I worked with Sarah using many of this book's exercises to create a unified culture. The workshops were immensely powerful in bringing the entire organization together. And now you have the opportunity to take advantage of them too!"

KIT COLBERT, former chief technology officer at VMware

"*Driving Outcomes* is a valuable companion for both new and seasoned leaders navigating significant change. Sarah Plantenberg draws from her vast experience to not only help you change culture but also develop resilient cultures. Through relevant and engaging first-person anecdotes, she helps you understand everyone's role in fostering a productive environment and aligning teams to drive business results."

OPAL PERRY, senior technical executive

"Sarah Plantenberg demystifies one of the prime components of organizational DNA: corporate culture. What it is, how it works, how to recognize it, and—most importantly—how to change it to attain desired business outcomes. *Driving Outcomes* is a must-read for anyone involved in corporate change management. Sarah provides the tools and techniques to help create a work environment where individuals and teams are aligned to—and driven by—business strategy."

MARC OUELLETTE, senior IT executive, technical strategy and implementation

"*Driving Outcomes* is an impactful culture story, a model for creating a healthy and productive culture, and a powerful resource for guiding your team toward that culture. Sarah Plantenberg presents both the 'why'—proof that a healthy culture drives performance—and the 'how'—actionable models and exercises to build consensus and confidence in that culture. If you lead a team that struggles with delivering on performance promises, this book is a must-read."

S. CHRIS EDMONDS, author of *The Culture Engine* and co-author of *Good Comes First*

"Sarah Plantenberg expertly identifies the pitfalls that dilute results and provides actionable strategies to align teams. Sarah's emphasis on culture as a strategic asset is both refreshing and vital; it's a critical reminder that success is not merely about metrics, but also about the human connections and values that underpin them. This book gives you the tools you need to masterfully lead at the intersection of human beings and technology."

STEVEN LEIST, chief technology officer

Driving
Outcomes

PAGE TWO

Driving Outcomes

How to Accelerate Business Results Through Culture

SARAH PLANTENBERG

Copyright © 2025 by Sarah Plantenberg

All rights reserved. No part of this book may be reproduced, stored in a retrieval system or transmitted, in any form or by any means, without the prior written consent of the publisher, except in the case of brief quotations, embodied in reviews and articles.

Some names and identifying details have been changed to protect the privacy of individuals.

Cataloguing in publication information is available from Library and Archives Canada.
ISBN 978-1-77458-560-3 (paperback)
ISBN 978-1-77458-567-2 (ebook)

Page Two
pagetwo.com

Edited by Brooke White
Copyedited by Crissy Boylan
Proofread by Alison Strobel
Cover and interior design by Jennifer Lum
Cover illustration by Allan Chu

driving-outcomes.com

*With deepest gratitude to the Most Holy Trinity.
May I always be a vessel of the Holy Spirit.*

---

*This book is for all those who, over the years,
taught me how to help them. The classroom only teaches so much,
and really it was only 25 percent of what I needed. You grew me
into the contributor I am today. I am profoundly grateful to
every user, individual contributor, manager, director, VP, CTO,
and CIO for what you taught me about reeling from, thriving in,
and driving change. I respect you. I admire you. I thank you.*

Contents

Introduction The Rhythm of Adaptation *1*
The Symmetry of a Coordinated Response *5*

1 Anatomy of a Team in Trouble *9*
Team Dynamics *10*
The Players: A Software Squad *14*
The Assignment: Innovation Differentiation *16*
The Problem: Competing Priorities and Unclear Outcomes *17*
The Solution: Orchestrating a Cultural Overhaul *19*

2 The Critical Interplay Between Culture and Outcomes *27*
What Is Culture? *28*
What Is an Outcome? *29*
So That: A Method to Clarify Outcomes *31*
Connecting Outcomes to People *45*

3 **The Human Factor** *47*
   The Role of Identity *49*
   Ripples of Change *50*
   Visibility for You *54*
   Your Brain on Threat *56*

4 **The Invisible Maze** *65*
   Catalysts of Friction *67*
   The Terrible Role Model *78*

5 **Designing Culture Change** *89*
   The Three Pillars of Cultural Alignment *91*
   The Contract for Change:
   Behavioral Norms from the Inside Out *102*

6 Catalysts for Culture Change Are Everywhere *105*
   Negative Bias Amplifies Friction *106*
   Inside Out: Catalysts from the Team *108*
   Outside In: External Catalysts *110*
   First Bank of Old Family Money: Internal and External Catalysts *121*

7 Leadership: The Most Important Ingredient for Culture *127*
   Servant Leadership *129*
   The Leadership To-Do List *138*
   Common Pitfalls *142*

8 Know Before You Grow: How to Seed a Deep-Rooted Culture *147*
   There Will Be Misalignment *149*
   Embrace the Constraints *152*
   Look Forward, Not Backward *158*
   Relationship Repair Through Trust Building *163*

9 Culture Begets Culture *171*
   The Squad Six Months Out *172*

Conclusion   **Be Inspired** *179*

Exercises   **Fourteen Activities for Culture Change** *181*

    The Benefits of "Working at the Wall" *182*

    Working with Ideas *185*

    The Flow *186*

    Exercise 1:   Hopes and Fears *192*

    Exercise 2:   Empathy Map *196*

    Exercise 3:   Active Listening *201*

    Exercise 4:   So That Method *203*

    Exercise 5:   So That Cascade *205*

    Exercise 6:   Business Impact Worksheet *209*

    Exercise 7:   Future Impact Article *221*

    Exercise 8:   Team Purpose *225*

    Exercise 9:   People Vision *229*

    Exercise 10: Values *235*

    Exercise 11: Contract for Change *238*

    Exercise 12: Doable Versus Valuable *241*

    Exercise 13: Contrarian Thinking *244*

    Exercise 14: Ideation *246*

Acknowledgments *249*

INTRODUCTION

The Rhythm of Adaptation

IMAGINE YOU'RE the owner of a suite of products. The type of industry doesn't matter. It could be hospitality, financial, retail—take your pick. Your job is to ensure the growth of the product line through the value delivered to your customers. As part of the business cycle, the heads of all the product suites, along with finance, marketing, and others, come together for annual planning sessions. In these sessions, product leaders discuss the strategy for their product suites over the next two years and decide on the budgets.

At this year's annual planning session, there's a new staffer on the leadership team. Arty's name has come up in phone calls and in hallway conversations for several months. Some of the senior executives have spent time with him, but this is the first time you and your peers will interact with him. In the past, you and your peers have looked at analyst reports, market research, and reviewed past customer activity looking for signals of their future choices. You've placed thoughtful bets about where to invest. As the meeting gets underway, you sense Arty has already had some influence on the strategic direction of the discussion. Nothing is wrong necessarily, but things are different.

This meeting is kicking off with a clearer image of the future than in years past, substantiated by quite a bit of data beyond the traditional market research and analysis reports from the leadership team, which Arty seems to understand deeply and recites back effortlessly. He is introducing data from sources no one had previously thought to consider but which are proving to be quite valuable. He is finding relationships in the data the team hadn't seen before and providing predictive analytics no one else in the company knows how to do. He's also considered the last five years of press releases and announcements from the competition, their strengths and weaknesses, and the areas of the market they seem to be focusing on. With all this data, Arty has simulated several scenarios that include risk analysis and projected outcomes. And he's delivered a prioritized list of strategic portfolio changes, additions, and integrations.

Let's pause here for a moment and look inward. What feelings come up when you witness Arty's contributions? Excitement? Apprehension? Put yourself in the shoes of someone who came to the table thinking you were prepared, only to see Arty's work. Might there be a little envy? Or fear? Perhaps you're curious about his incredible skills. Where did he come from? Maybe you're discreetly Googling him on your phone under the conference room table, trying to get more information.

Surely, responses to Arty will be mixed. In just one meeting, he has shifted everyone's roles in different ways. That much is evident.

Until Arty's role is made clear, there will be friction. That friction can take many forms and will persist until everyone understands what Arty's contributions mean for their roles and how the changes he suggests will impact them. If this situation is handled well, understanding and trust will eventually grease the skids, and people will be able to move freely again. Until then, people will be anxious to know:

- What they can expect from Arty
- How they are expected (or how they desire) to contribute to Arty's efforts
- What changes in the business or its goals have necessitated Arty and his role
- How their own roles have changed
- If they should be aware of, expect, or work toward new or different outcomes

With this information, the team can revise their goals and set up communication and performance measurement structures that support reaching those goals. In other words, what Arty means for *them* will become clear, and they can again work with confidence and clarity.

Arty is a metaphor for artificial intelligence (corny name, I know). I've introduced new technologies (Arty-type figures), methodologies, and process changes many times throughout my career, and every time these things are introduced, they introduce culture changes, which are invisible to most of the people affected. People love the *idea* of improvements promised by new technologies or methodologies yet hesitate to do everything necessary to fully adopt them. An invisible maze of friction points inhibits their commitment to change.

People are fearful when they cannot see or do not understand how their roles and value will change as a result of adopting a new technology or methodology. Obviously, they can't proceed as usual, but what is next? Should they invest their time and energy in this new technology or method, or will leadership eventually abandon the new initiative, as they have done with others, several times in the past? Is this a proactive change intended to drive new outcomes, and if so, what are those outcomes? Or are we closing a gap? How will people know what to start and stop doing because of these changes? How will people know when they are successful?

These are just a few examples of questions the team needed answered to smoothly integrate with Arty without slowing down the pace of business. These questions strike at the heart of what motivates people in the workplace: vision, purpose, feeling valued, and what to do next. They point to both personal and professional identity.

I've worked with small teams made up of a handful of people as well as organizations rolling out change to thousands. The more people involved, the more sentiment around change is amplified. When change initiatives are clearly communicated and widely accepted, great! People are engaged, innovation flows, and the positivity can be seen in business outcomes. But when dozens to thousands of people are frustrated by blindly feeling their way through an invisible maze of unclear outcomes, the dominoes fall: misalignment, negativity, feeling devalued or at risk, and disengagement. Imagine these two different sentiments and their impacts magnified throughout your organization—only one will strengthen your business.

A goal of all organizations, regardless of size, should be to create a culture that proactively senses and responds to its own changing needs to stay competitive and efficient. Part of those changing needs includes the needs of the human beings. Human beings do the work, and lack of clarity slows down progress, inhibiting the achievement of business outcomes. It seems simple enough, on the surface, for those introducing Arty to say:

> Meet Arty. His role is to leverage big data and predictive analytics to help us develop strategies to stay in Gartner's Magic Quadrant. Arty will deliver XYZ artifacts from which we will make decisions. You will lead your product teams through the execution of these strategies and provide feedback and input back into Arty's department. Good? Good.

The Symmetry of a Coordinated Response

Why isn't this a sufficient introduction to a new technology? Because we're dealing with human beings. Intertwined with the decision-making that goes into doing their jobs are their very human needs, desires, values, and emotions, plus the wisdom they've gained over their lifetimes, however long or short. Inside these human beings lies a primitive brain, whose response reflex is faster than the more recently formed (evolutionarily speaking) executive function. That primitive brain doesn't know the difference between a new employee who may disrupt their position or a charging grizzly bear. A threat is a threat, and here comes the response! We'll dissect the responses and their impacts on your business throughout the book, but they are disruptive.

With introspection, individuals can usually manage their primitive responses in a productive manner, provided they receive the right information about how they will be impacted by proposed changes. And ideally they work in a culture that supports and values the personal work required to do so.

What happens when a team or organization must come to their own conclusions about change and how it will impact them? I'll ask the question this way: When you imagine your team responding to change, would you like it to a school of fish—everyone is shifting as one organism—or would you like it to a swarm of gnats—everyone is chaotically reacting to different input, zigzagging this way and that? In case it wasn't clear, you want the fish.

Negativity amplifies within a system, causing churn. It can cost much more to produce the same results, and worse yet, productivity and quality wane. Response to change must be coordinated if you want it to be productive and efficient.

In the pages ahead, I share what I have learned about the impact of culture on human beings and ultimately business outcomes, from my decades of working with individuals and organizations traversing the disruptions of new technology, market, and cultural changes. I've developed a system to meaningfully advance your culture to both improve those outcomes and how you achieve them. This includes the inner workings of human beings: how they think and feel, what motivates them and what harms them. In that work, I discovered that human beings, culture, and ever-changing goals together make a dynamic system. The way this system functions directly impacts, if not determines, business outcomes.

This book examines the interplay of human cognitive and emotional factors, the power structures, and the business processes that are constantly at play in organizations, revealing the common pitfalls and friction points that slow down teamwork and bifurcate efforts, ultimately diluting your business results.

You will learn practical techniques to intentionally design the team and organizational cultures to create the right conditions for your company-specific outcomes. The concepts presented here will enable you to mine for conflict, amplify synergies, identify opportunities to organically improve relationships, align goals and values, and strengthen communication. The resulting new culture will remove roadblocks and drive alignment across priorities to direct talent, create momentum, and accelerate business results. Specific attention is paid to identifying friction as soon as it begins so it can be removed.

Getting results is easier than you might think. I've included exercises in the back of this book to help you start realizing change; you will see relevant activities mentioned in specific sections of the book.

You can use these exercises in a few ways:

- Individually to develop personal insights about yourself and your motivations

- In pairs to work through areas of conflict or repair after difficulties

- In small groups to develop a better understanding of synergies and pitfalls within the team as a system

- For the highest effectiveness, in a workshop setting at the team, the organization, or the company-wide leadership level (with you or an external consultant as facilitator)

To go after culture change in a coordinated fashion across one or more systems, you will want to run a workshop. Workshops include many of the activities in the back of the book, along with additional activities and facilitation instructions for doing this work with groups. The more people who engage together in a coordinated fashion, the more profound your outcomes will be.

I believe deeply in this work. I've devoted my life to helping people work together better—whole, complete people, not just your "work selves," because it's the entire person who shows up every day. The exercises in this book will give you the tools to reduce friction caused by blind spots, assumptions, misalignment, and divergent ways of working. If you and those around you choose to work the activities in this book, you can build trust and quickly overcome the hurt caused by working in environments riddled with friction. Most important to me is that you have less occasion to protect those aspects of you that make you human: your desires, fears, and sense of identity.

My dream outcome for this book is a revolution in workplace culture: en masse, workplaces would understand the intersections of culture and business outcomes and commit to fluidly adapting to change, for the sake of the business and out of appreciation and respect for the human beings who make up that business.

Change happens all the time—and at a faster rate than ever before. *Driving Outcomes* is designed to help you anticipate and prepare for it, so you can leverage the right leadership style to maintain the rhythm of adaptation, no matter what comes your way.

1

Anatomy of a Team in Trouble

Culture eats strategy for breakfast.
PETER DRUCKER

THE SOFTWARE design team was surprised and pleased to have their outstanding first-quarter accomplishments recognized at an organization-wide meeting. They had clearly demonstrated they could deliver innovation, increase team productivity, and improve key operational metrics such as speed to market, reduced defects, and lower costs. What no one knew was that only three months before the meeting, the team had been coming apart at the seams. A cascade of problems threatened the team's long-term viability:

- Misaligned values
- Unclear goals
- Imperiled psychological safety
- Building resentment
- Impaired productivity

The values of the team members and of their leadership were at odds. Because the values were unspoken, the misalignment was invisible; the team could only sense something was wrong when friction crept in and impacted workflow and morale. The project outcomes and goals were unclear: when it came time to make decisions, the team churned. Leadership assumed the problems were with process and performance. They increased pressure to perform, which chipped away at the psychological safety of the team. The less safe the team felt, the more resentful and invisible they felt and the less productive they became. Many team members dreaded coming to work and struggled to accomplish even the most basic of tasks. The team was in a downward spiral with no end in sight.

Software design is a cross-functional effort, meaning people from different disciplines collaborate throughout the product lifecycle to create the software people use every day. In the case of enterprises, we're talking either about an IT organization internal to a business or an enterprise software company. Enterprise IT organizations buy, build, and run the software that operates the (enterprise, or very big) company. All enterprises have them: banks, airlines, insurance companies, hospitals, hotels, grocery stores, and the list goes on. Enterprise software companies build and sell software to enterprises. These are companies like my alma mater, IBM, or Dell, Oracle, and so on.

Team Dynamics

To better understand the predicament and successful turnaround of the software team in our story, let me give you context into their dynamics, working environment, and how this company wound up in its predicament. All these pieces are important to understand why it's so critical to create the right conditions for teams to succeed in driving outcomes, as well as why it's so important to keep those outcomes current.

Our team works in the IT department of an international hotel, which we'll call Always Home Hotels. The IT organization is based in San Francisco, with several remote employees in other areas of the world. Always Home is over seventy years old. When it started, Always Home's brand was about the comfort of home while away from home. In the 1950s when Always Home was born, staying in a hotel meant a certain level of pampering. Whether you were a business traveler unwinding after a day of work or a family on their annual vacation, you had maid and room service at your fingertips and restaurants, pools, and tennis courts just outside your door.

The amenities in hotels were lovely, though the experience came with a certain amount of disruption, precisely because people were not in their own homes. Families with children, in particular, dealt with the inconveniences of the whole family living in one room, especially when children were too young to have an adjoining room, packing medications for every possibility, enough diapers and supplies for at least the first few days, coping with dirty laundry for a whole family, and so on. This disruption was simply part of taking a vacation.

About thirty years into its life, Always Home spotted a trend in the market—specific amenities for guests staying five or more days, or "extended stay" guests. Hotels added laundry facilities on each floor, renovated rooms to include separate sleeping and lounging areas, and equipped rooms with either fully functioning kitchens or kitchenettes. Other amenities also included happy hours with light fare and self-serve breakfast buffets. Some hotels changed all their rooms into extended stay rooms, and some opened locations specifically designed and branded for longer-term travelers. (As a consultant, I made ample use of this lovely combination of preparing my own meals while on the road and someone cleaning up after me!) This option became popular with families throughout the 1990s and early 2000s thanks to the great blend of better use of space, cost-saving opportunities, and housekeeping.

It's important to know that at this time hotels were only competing with other hotels, and they all ran their businesses in pretty much the same way. Employees and salespeople looking for a change or promotion simply moved from one hotel to another. All the hotel leaders saw the world roughly through the same lens, used the same vendors, and saw each other at the same conventions. Big moves happened far less frequently than today and were relatively easy to respond to.

Then came Airbnb, which flung the doors wide open and allowed anyone to make a room, a guest house, or their entire home and property available. This was so disruptive to the hospitality industry that it is still redefining itself. My favorite part of this disruption is that Airbnb is a technology company, not a hotel chain. Airbnb owns no property. Rather, its founders saw an opportunity to connect hosts and travelers and designed a platform to do just that. Airbnb made a software application that puts power into the hands of guests to search and find the exact property, location, and amenities that meets their needs. This is a major paradigm shift to which, in my opinion, traditional hotels simply cannot respond in kind. They need to reinvent themselves, but that's a different book.

What you need to know to understand Always Home's situation is that Airbnb became more appealing than Always Home to families and young non-business travelers. Always Home (along with many others in the hospitality industry) did not predict the impact Airbnb would have on its business, specifically the paradigm shifts for customers who now had every possible option at their fingertips. Over the last decade, this area of the hotel's business had declined. Not only were these specific demographics opting for Airbnb, but the end-to-end experience of Airbnb is more modern, gives customers more options and control, and results in a highly personalized experience.

Now that we have some insight into what ails Always Home Hotels, let's understand the software team working on behalf of the hotel to address the loss in market share. Software teams can be as few as a dozen people or made up of hundreds to thousands of people. It all depends on the size of the company and the size of the software application. The software squad in this story is fifteen people strong: six designers, six developers, one anchor or lead developer, the product manager, and engineering architect. They were in an innovation center tasked with experimenting with emerging technology and identifying new opportunities for the business. When the innovation team hit on something valuable, the discovery would be absorbed by an existing product organization outside the innovation center. There were several squads within the innovation center, experimenting with different emerging technologies. Overall, the innovation team had two layers: the executive layer and what I call the "doer" layer. For the doers, the innovation center was their entire job. For the executives, the innovation center was one of many areas of focus within the IT department.

The Players: A Software Squad

To assist in understanding the personalities, expertise, and responsibility dynamics within our software squad, I've created a cast of characters complete with job titles and key areas of focus. The following descriptions of some of the doers and executives are highly abridged to provide enough information so you can understand the nuances of the story and the squad's challenges as they unfold.

The Doers

The people who are hands-on-keyboard, designing, developing, and testing the software.

Carlos: the engineering architect, responsible for making sure that both application infrastructure and architecture decisions are extensible into existing products so innovations can be easily assumed into the business with little to no technical debt.

Jiang: the lead developer who leads one of the many software squads in the innovation center. He is the anchor for a team of six developers working on this project.

Mei: the product owner, responsible for envisioning and planning the project and its value to the business and its users. Mei is technically not part of the software squad because she owns multiple projects, whereas squads are assigned to one project at a time. But Mei is an honorary squad member when she is actively working with the squad.

Jeffrey: the senior designer, responsible for collaborating with Jiang, Mei, and Carlos, specifically at the envisioning stage. He then works with the design team to get the project off the ground. Jeffrey also oversees the design and user testing.

Jo: the lead designer, runs the day-to-day, works with Arun to break their work into smaller tasks (called "stories"), and communicates to Jeffrey and Mei how much effort the stories will require (also referred to as the "size").

Arun: the early career designer, mostly works on components or individual pages or collaborates with Jo to design larger workflows. He is not involved in planning or strategic work.

The Executives

The people responsible for how technology and user experience impact the strategic direction and growth of the company, as well as for running the overall disciplines of engineering, product ownership, and design.

Carol: vice president (VP) of Software, oversees all technical innovation and its impact on the overall business.

Ethan: chief technology officer (CTO), responsible for ensuring the company is aware of emerging technology and its benefits in a timely manner. He responds accordingly by leveraging the right technology at the right time and in the right way.

Barry: VP of Product, responsible for ensuring products are leading in the market, retiring products that are no longer of value to the business, and identifying opportunities for business growth.

Melanie: VP of Design, responsible for creative and experience strategies that drive end-to-end product experiences, as well as strong cohesion to brand identity.

Emma: senior design manager, not technically an executive, but she bridges Melanie and Jeffrey. Emma's role is to ensure the design team has everything they need to do their jobs, and she is ultimately responsible for their growth and impact.

You will hear about these individuals throughout the book, so I present you with the whole cast of characters now. All names, titles, locations, and the details of specific situations have been changed. I've worked with thousands of people throughout my career, so if you recognize a familiar anecdote, know that you're one of many, many people who have faced similar situations. I wrote this book because the patterns across teams and industries are so very strong.

At its core, this book is about how human beings respond to change when it feels threatening or confusing, and there is every distraction and obfuscation to which a person can cling, to feel like they are making progress. So yes, it's about you, and it's about me. It's about us and how we can intentionally build cultures that usher us through change.

The Assignment: Innovation Differentiation

Our doers—Jeffrey (senior designer), Jo (lead designer), Arun (designer), Jiang (lead developer), Mei (product owner), and Carlos (architect)—were given the assignment to reimagine their company's role in the hospitality market, specifically to draw back the waning demographics of young non-business travelers and families. They asked the team to develop concepts that used AI to drive personalized experiences. Carol (VP of Software) wanted to report back to the board of directors that she'd accomplished two goals. First, she had leveraged cutting-edge technology, cementing the hotel as an innovation leader. Second, she could use this technology to bring back the family and non-business travelers.

Over the last decade, the company had slowly slid backward, losing touch with the needs of modern users. Impatiently, it sacrificed big strategic moves for getting features out the door quickly. Those features were usually directed toward satisfying one or two large customers, helping close large deals with corporate customers, and boosting revenue metrics. But they weren't moving the business forward in a substantial way, nor were these features keeping Always Home competitive. While still considered an industry leader by analysts, hotel room sales and usage among some demographics that had been showing ominous signs of slowing for years were now visibly problematic to the board of directors. In short, Always Home had lost touch with its younger demographics. Ironically, the very moves Always Home made to improve revenue contributed to the problem.

After two years of working to mold, shape, and define an innovative concept, the software squad's progress on the project looked very promising. It had become the darling of the organization and key to the business's future. Typically, at this point, the project would be assumed into another business unit to stabilize the product and ready it for market. Shifting the concept out of the innovation center and into a business unit organized to own a software application for the long run often means a temporary slowdown in progress, while the new designers and developers come up to speed on everything.

The Problem: Competing Priorities and Unclear Outcomes

To maintain speed to market, Carol made the decision to keep the project inside the innovation center, keep the team intact, and put Barry (VP of Product), Melanie (VP of Design), and Ethan (CTO) in charge of bringing her new baby to market.

Over several months of working to bring this concept to market, I'd watched morale wane as priorities shifted, sometimes multiple times in one day, without clarity as to why. As a consultant, I had been working with the innovation center teams and with this software squad quite closely on the adoption of lean, agile methodologies. Lean, agile methods are designed to help teams respond quickly to changing priorities, but not when that change is without rhyme or reason. They are anchored in alignment of shared priorities, driven by bringing value to the customer. In this situation, there was a lack of clarity across the team, which (we will soon see) came from the top. Because people could not settle on what to build or what the outcomes were, the squad was churning.

At the root of the problem were competing priorities: the members of the executive leadership team were all imagining different outcomes for the project based on their roles. In her mind's eye, Carol was seeing big headlines splashed across *Forbes* and *Wired* touting new market shifts based on the project. Barry, feeling like Always Home was stuck in a game of parity with the competition, was thinking about leapfrogging out of this game and putting everyone in the rearview mirror. Ethan was trying to be practical about how to deliver something useful quickly, while laying the groundwork for future releases. Melanie (VP of Design) saw design in a supportive role. She instructed her team to press Barry's team for requirements. Emma (senior design manager) was in the best position to make a difference because she was hands-on with the squad on a regular basis. (Remember, the innovation team usually hands off their projects. This time, it was kept in-house, meaning the team needed additional processes.) This gave her opportunities to show people how best to work in a streamlined manner. However, because the problem started higher up than Emma, the churn continued.

In my role as a consultant, my focus was educating people on the methodologies. It was not within the purview of my contract to build alignment between Carol and her executive leadership. Nor would that have been welcomed. My leadership was aware that mid-contract, Carol decided this innovation squad would become the owners of this technology, instead of another business unit. My marching orders for working with this big change were to do the best I could within the boundaries of the contract. However, I've built, grown, and managed many teams, and I could clearly see the executives were functioning within their silos, not as a single leadership team. Eventually, the doers' productivity sagged, and they started pushing against each other as they reflected the desires of their siloed leaders. The doers asked to speak to me in private to see if I could help, which was technically outside the scope of my contract. Some confided they were looking for work elsewhere. Contract or not, my conscience required I do what I could.

To help right the ship, I reached out to Melanie and Emma and offered to run a few exercises specifically designed to help the team triage, repair damage, and get back on track. They agreed, and within three months, values were aligned, fractures were on the way to repair, and the team took control of driving the culture they needed to thrive.

The Solution: Orchestrating a Cultural Overhaul

What happened? I leveraged the insights and exercises in this book. Having worked at the intersection of human beings and technology for over twenty-five years—first as a software designer; then as a designer of business strategies, digital transformation, and internal organizational structures; and finally as an innovator of technology and methodology—I have worked with thousands of people and dozens of organizations. My discipline is human factors. Part of my work includes helping businesses understand certain aspects of human beings so they can make more valuable products that are a delight to use and that build strong relationships—what businesses call "loyalty." I don't use that term often because it's incomplete. "Relationship" is a more accurate term than "loyalty" because it speaks to the connection between the two entities. Good relationships are built on honesty, trustworthiness, and mutual respect. I hope these themes come through clearly as you read, because they also apply to the human beings that make up the business and define a company's culture. You can quickly reset your culture—even when negativity has taken hold—to one in which people are thriving and driving your business outcomes.

The approach I use consists of a three-pronged strategy:

1 Getting crystal clear on business outcomes and the purpose behind those outcomes

2 Working with teams to make sure each person is aligned to the overall outcomes and understands their contributions

3 Defining the values necessary to ensure the personal and organizational contributions take place with ease and with minimal conflict

I usually start with one team within a squad (design, product management, or development) to create a fully functioning, healthy group with concrete organizational goals and outcomes. Critical to this initiative is ensuring leadership provides clear direction and focus for their team. From there, we extend the work outward to include others.

You can quickly reset your culture to one in which people are thriving and driving your business outcomes

———————

In this case, the first thing I did was work with the design team to clearly align on their design goals and identify what was needed to reach those goals. The people involved were Jeffrey, Jo, Arun, Emma, and Melanie. You'll notice this group was made up of both doers and executives, so we had two layers of people involved with different responsibilities for the design team, all of which rolled up to the overall outcomes.

Different responsibilities add slightly different layers of purpose. Think of it like whitewater rafting. Everyone in the raft is paddling, but the person in the back is steering. Their work looks similar, but they are making a unique contribution to help the team get from A to B.

From my vantage point, I saw everyone was making assumptions about each other's roles. We needed to get clear on exactly how people expected the design team to function, what the outcomes were, and what the team members needed to achieve those outcomes. To do this, we needed a deep understanding of each person's motivations, values, and needs. We looked for synergies and areas where misalignment created dysfunction. As we embarked upon this work, there was misalignment everywhere, which prohibited the team from achieving their outcomes. Everyone was frustrated or in downright emotional pain. Unmet needs by both the doers and the leaders led to mistrust, and no one knew how to remedy the situation. The team was melting down.

As we moved through the workshop, in short order the team started to see what I saw; they could see beyond the friction to *why* it existed. Melanie, in particular, became acutely aware of the environment she and her executive counterparts, Barry and Ethan, were creating for the whole team. The lack of executive alignment resulted in the cross-functional team members feeling as if they were pitted against each other, each struggling for the power to achieve their own outcome, as modeled by their leadership. After all, the teams within the squad were evaluated quarterly by their leadership. Barry, Ethan, and Melanie would all be measuring how successful their teams were at helping them achieve their own goals. We might call this a cross-*dysfunctional* team.

As the dysfunction continued, frustration snowballed. Week after week, the design team's productivity and quality were declining. Melanie was downright angry and pressured Emma to get the team back in shape. And Emma was angry because the team didn't do what she told them to do.

Moreover, once the project became officially theirs, Jeffrey, Jo, and Arun felt they had been inundated with process. There was more administrative work to do, filling out reports, and making slides for monthly executive meetings. They had not been so close to the executive ranks for a project before, and they didn't understand the value these activities brought. To them, it was silly executive busywork. Both Jeffrey and Jo were so unhappy and felt so stuck, they were talking about leaving the organization. You've heard the saying "People don't leave companies, they leave managers." Well, that was where we were headed.

Once Melanie understood her role in frustrating her team's efforts, she was able to make immediate changes. Melanie set up time with Barry and Ethan to see how she might help influence alignment. And with Emma's help, they were able to give Jeffrey, Jo, and Arun insight into the value this "busywork" provided for the team, specifically by reporting team productivity up to Carol. The team's impact and productivity provided credibility for the entire discipline of design in the innovation center and helped procure additional funding for the broader team. Melanie was also able to show the brand equity gained with customers when the design team did usability testing and pulled customer feedback into the product. With this insight, Jeffrey, Jo, and Arun stopped complaining about the administrative work and even found ways to automate it to create more efficiencies for themselves and to provide Melanie with cleaner data.

Basically, we were merging values across the two levels of the design team, while at the same time understanding that because we had doers and leadership, there would be *differences in values* caused by the different jobs they did. We see this in complex teams where many different groups work together. (More on this variance in Chapter 6.) With values either aligned or differences understood, we can move on to addressing psychological safety, as these two go together. In every culture workshop I've led, someone lists the values of trust and respect. The design team expressed those needs as well, and you can see why. Assumptions led to people blaming each other, which exacerbated the problem. For leaders, blaming anyone, inside or outside your team, is a great way to lose credibility and the respect of your subordinates. I want to be crystal clear on this point: leaders are expected to get to the bottom of problems and provide resources or conditions for change to take place, which is different than blaming. (More on this in Chapter 8.) The realignment that comes with clarity around purpose and values is part of the solution. The rest is about creating psychological safety, repairing relationships, and creating optimal conditions in which trust can exist. Building this foundation or repairing an existing foundation takes time, but if everyone is clear on the goals and committed to them, we can get there faster than you might think.

Getting to psychological safety can be different for everyone. Requirements for psychological safety are shaped by several factors, not the least of which is people's personal backgrounds. The design team was composed of people from several countries. Jeffrey was born, raised, and lived in Austin, Texas. Arun had relocated to San Francisco from Pune, India, and Jo lived in a multigenerational household in Beijing.

In Jo's culture, it was very inappropriate to challenge or even question leadership. However, in her role, she was expected to challenge ideas in ways that put her professional identity in conflict with her personal identity. Jo could have an honest exchange of ideas with Jeffrey, but she would never contradict or express dissatisfaction to Emma, Melanie, Carlos, or anyone significantly above her. Jo had to juggle cultures daily. Stepping outside her comfort zone felt unsafe.

Emma, in San Francisco but born and raised in Brooklyn, had been in technology a long time. For the first fifteen years of her career, she was the only woman in the room. Her points of view were often dismissed or passed off as someone else's. To be heard, she learned to over-rotate, speak loudly, talk over her male counterparts, and use severe language—behaviors Emma never shed because they had been so effective. To the design team, Emma seemed like a dictator who intentionally created a culture of fear.

Can you see how Jo's and Emma's personalities and backgrounds could create a downward spiral of fear (for Jo) and frustration (for Emma)? And we haven't even touched on Melanie's background! Everyone's different needs and requirements can easily create a logjam of unsafety. In the face of fear, people shut down. Once we get our minds around people's needs, which can happen in just a couple hours, we can design a culture that considers everyone. This breaks up the logjam, and the team is back to paddling through the rapids.

In our workshop, we used several exercises in this book to help people understand each other's needs, repair relationships, and build new behavioral norms based on shared values.

We then got explicit about behavior changes by writing down what people would do to maintain the changes to which the team had agreed, along with what people would *stop* doing. I call this a contract. (More on that tool in the exercises at the end of the book.) While the catalysts for many of the team's problems lay with the leadership, we made sure to remove as many contributing and exacerbating behaviors as possible.

I then instituted regular retrospectives to help people as they built new habits. Retrospectives are a practice of examining team progress on, well, just about anything! The practice of meeting weekly to review progress or setbacks gives everyone a chance to look at themselves and revisit the commitments they made in the contract. Consistent and well-run retrospectives also help restore trust, which in turn rebuilds psychological safety.

As this work unfolds, resentment naturally subsides because people understand each other better. Assumptions are replaced by empathy and supportive action. What we get as a result is a high-functioning team, deeply attuned to one another. In other words, what we get is a productive and vibrant culture, clear on the desired business outcomes and how to make choices to get those outcomes.

2

The Critical Interplay Between Culture and Outcomes

Culture isn't just one aspect of the game, it is the game. In the end, an organization is nothing more than the collective capacity of its people to create value.
LOUIS V. GERSTNER JR.

WHAT *IS* CULTURE, and how do we craft this invisible force in complex environments filled with many kinds of people and fast-changing priorities? The first anthropological definition of culture comes from nineteenth-century British anthropologist Edward Burnett Tylor: "Culture... is that complex whole which includes knowledge, belief, art, law, morals, custom, and any other capabilities and habits acquired by man as a member of society."

What Is Culture?

For business purposes, I will take a pragmatic approach and define culture as *the expression of what is truly valued in an organization*. Read in this definition such factors as:

- How people decide what is spoken and when to be silent
- The ways in which people speak to each other
- How decisions are made
- What people act on and what is ignored
- What is measured and not measured
- What is celebrated (success or suffering)

Where people put their attention and energy signals what they value and the expected behavioral norms. Despite what may be written in company values or culture statements, anyone observing a team for some time will be able to describe that team's culture. How much it matches company statements is a separate matter.

I love this summary from "The Impact of Leadership Styles on Organizational Culture and Firm Effectiveness: An Empirical Study" by Andrew S. Klein, Joseph Wallis, and Robert A. Cooke in the *Journal of Management and Organization*: "An organizational culture emerges as a collective creation of members' interaction with others as they strive to make sense of their environment." What stands out to me in this quote is the word "emerge." Culture is not a statement we make; it's both how we act and what motivates that action. It's collective. There is a feedback loop between culture and people.

Human beings make choices based on their values, their organization's values, or both. These choices ripple out into the organization as work, conversations or silence, accountability or lack thereof. They impact the people around you and business outcomes. These impacts send signals rippling back into the organization. They can be positive (we achieved all our goals within budget, or a team celebration of a job well done) or negative (we missed some goals, we blew out our budget, or hard work goes unacknowledged). How people respond to positive and negative news is feedback into the culture loop.

Of note, a positive business outcome does not always equate to a positive impact on culture. Recall our software squad. The product was released on time even though Jo, Jeffrey, and Arun had less time to do their jobs than they should have had due to the churn among executives. This was because they worked nights and weekends. Leadership was aware of the overwork but never let up on the pressure. They sent a negative signal to the team, which was that their personal time was not valued.

What we are looking for is alignment. We want clearly defined outcomes, values that drive honest motivation inside every individual in relation to that outcome, and strong leadership that sets the tone. When all is aligned, people's talents, knowledge, and wisdom make their way into the organizational system, generating a positive cultural feedback loop.

What Is an Outcome?

An outcome is *the consequence of an action or series of actions*. For outcomes to be achieved, they must be coherent and of value to the business. Business owners: be aware that your outcomes will be different from your customers' outcomes. Yet your outcomes are contingent on providing your customers with their outcomes. There are many variances between your customers' outcomes and yours, and they may not all be under your control. Critical to building your business on a solid foundation is getting really crisp on these three things:

1. Your business outcomes
2. The relationships between your business outcomes and your customers' outcomes
3. The contributions of everyone on the team (or in the broader organization—you can scale this work to include the entire company)

Assumptions and gaps between these three things will interrupt your ability to achieve outcomes.

Think of assumptions like boulders placed in shallow water. As waves come to shore, their energy is broken and fragmented into sprays of water in all directions. In this case, the waves are the energy, time, and money invested in bringing something to market. When that energy hits an assumption, it's chaotically dispersed away from the outcome. Some of the wave (your investment) reaches the shore, and some is wasted. Your investment is also wasted when it dribbles into gaps that were invisible or, worse yet, ignored. This would be a culture of waste, of silos and mediocrity, a culture that does not value the company's investment or the investment of its employees' time and talent.

Close gaps and address assumptions by understanding the relationships between your outcomes, your customers' outcomes, and every individual's contribution. You may not be able to close every gap or address every assumption on your own, but you can go after the partnerships and information needed to do so. Design your culture to support outcomes that are built on a rock-solid foundation.

There are several common pitfalls when it comes to understanding outcomes, and they can be intertwined with each other, such as:

- Thinking only of your own business outcomes and forgetting about the dependencies: customers achieving their business outcomes promised by your product or service, sales teams, advertising, marketing, and so on
- Mistaking the end of a task or workflow for the outcome, whether it's yours or your customers' outcomes
- Conflating outcomes with metrics or key performance indicators (KPIs): the outcome is what happened because of your actions or product; metrics and KPIs signal the direction in which you are going
- Defining features, products, or services without being clear about how a customer's work or life is better after they engage with your product or service

So That: A Method to Clarify Outcomes

To get crystal clear on identifying business outcomes, I employ a commonly used technique known as the So That method. I did not invent this formula—it is a staple of the designer's toolkit—but the template I use looks like this:

> We will provide [person / people] with [product / feature / service] so that [outcome for your customer or your business—whichever you're working on at the moment].

Person / people: This is the target customer. If you're chasing multiple demographics, you'll define an outcome for each. You may want to go so far as to build personas, which will help you understand the unique needs and motivations of each demographic.

Product / feature / service: This is the thing you put into the world to make a difference in people's lives. In the for-profit world, you want to make this thing so valuable that people will part with their money to get the outcome it promises. You can get as granular as needed with this. Keep in mind: if you use this template for multiple layers (and you should!), everything should connect. For example, a feature within a product within a product suite (such as Microsoft Office).

Outcome: An outcome is not the completion of a task; it is the change that ensues during or after an event. If you are working on a customer outcome, this is the change that happens for the customer. This change may take place in a product or service, or it may take place *outside* a product or service. Second only to not doing the work of identifying outcomes, this is where the biggest mistakes are made. If you are working on your business outcomes, think beyond revenue. The more comprehensive you can be about what success looks like to your business, the fewer assumptions and gaps you will have.

The So That method helps you discover gaps in your business model, as well as places where you need thoughtful intersections with other areas of the business. Retrofitting existing business goals into this template can reveal that what you considered to be business outcomes are simply a series of activities that maintain the status quo, or are aimed at stopping the bleeding, instead of growing the business.

Carol, our VP of Software at the hotel, has two goals:

1. Creating personalized experiences for the hotel's target twenty-five- to thirty-five-year-old customers
2. Cementing the hotel as an innovation leader

Let's put Carol's first goal of creating personalized experiences for their different customer demographics into the template.

Research conducted by Barry (VP of Product) showed that the hotel did not meet the needs of nor feel relatable to non-business travelers between the ages of twenty-five to thirty-five. Furthermore, the hotel chain adds expense and inconvenience for young families. When the demographic of twenty-five- to thirty-five-year-olds thinks of hotels, they think of their parents. And that's exactly who Barry discovered likes Always Home. Business travelers and non-business travelers over the age of fifty-five preferred the predictability, services, and brand equity earned by large hotel chains over the years, while younger customers feel more at home in Airbnbs.

Here's an example of Always Home's template for their target customer's outcomes. We start with customer outcomes first to make sure your business is anchored in customer value.

> Always Home will provide customers ages twenty-five to thirty-five with personalized recommendations of hotel amenities, local restaurants, and events so that they have a more convenient, enriched experience, a more delightful stay, and feel Always Home Hotels understands them.

For this example, we're staying relatively high level. It is the responsibility of Mei and the design team to drill down into the "so that" portion of the statement to figure out exactly *what* to build to move the needle in that direction. A common misstep is that teams first align several steps down the road, on what service or product to provide. You can see why this is problematic: the product or service must deliver a customer outcome that hasn't been discussed or validated with the customer. At this point, you do not know if the outcome created by the product or service will be of value to the customer. This is one major point of churn. Teams iterate on products and services in an echo chamber, measuring success by arbitrary metrics. Some even settle on what to build based on what the highest-level executive likes, or because the clock ran out.

This template won't tell you what to build, but it will align everyone on customer outcomes throughout the product lifecycle. It will also surface for you what information you need to make good decisions.

Some things we can ascertain from the template are:

- Terms, such as "convenient, enriched experience, and a more delightful stay," came up in the research referenced by Barry. Because the Always Home team has lost touch with this demographic, they cannot rely on their interpretation of these words, especially since these words define success for the customer. These terms are best defined through research with the target demographic.

- What feeling "understood" by the hotel means to the demographic and ways to measure that experience are also best done through research—again, more clarity of this valued outcome from the customer point of view

- Possible rebranding, through marketing and communications (an acknowledgment that the hotel needs more than AI and software to solve the problem)

It's possible that the research uncovers other directions the hotel should go (which is why they adopted agile and lean methods), but for now, we will continue with this example.

Now that we have a starting place for Always Home's target customers, let's use the template to connect the executive team's business outcomes to the customer outcomes. The board is counting on Carol to stop the bleeding and recapture some of the hotel's market share. Therefore, Carol's business outcome is to increase market share of non-business travelers between the ages of twenty-five to thirty-five. Building on the customer outcomes, the template would look like this:

> Always Home will provide customers ages twenty-five to thirty-five with personalized recommendations of hotel amenities, local restaurants, and events so that they have a more convenient, enriched experience, a more delightful stay, and feel Always Home Hotels understands them, so that Always Home is considered a relevant brand to this market and recaptures these customers.

Grammatically, it's messy, but this clearly shows the relationships between customer and business outcomes. Honestly, this statement is a bit aspirational; Always Home lost a core demographic because they didn't keep up with the paradigm shift in the market. Some hotels might choose not to compete with Airbnb and instead focus on the demographics with whom they have strong relationships; Carol and the board of directors are not willing to let this demographic go without a fight. Will Always Home recapture this market in one fell swoop, by releasing an innovative idea powered by AI? Unlikely. But if they execute well and stay close to their customers throughout the process, they will move the needle.

Starting with the customer is the best catalyst for the paradigm shift that needs to occur.

Having said that, Always Home didn't do the So That statements. (I added them here for continuity.) Let's look at what really happened to illustrate how helpful So That statements *would have* been.

Barry and Mei discussed the AI concepts on the table. They chose what they thought Carol would like and felt confident presenting to analysts, the senior executives of their biggest customers, and the board of directors. Mei then pulled together a "happy path" slide deck about how she hoped the selected concept would improve Always Home's bottom line.

Ethan took a different approach. As the person holding the engineering headcount, he had the most control over getting a working product out the door, and everyone knew it. He took advantage of the fact that this part of the culture leaned in his favor, and he had decided, months earlier, how he would spend his budget. Under his guidance, his team was working on a few concepts to demonstrate their AI capabilities. To make his presentation to Carol as powerful as possible, he purchased some Airbnb data (yes, that data is available for purchase, but don't worry, it's anonymized) and asked Carlos to look at which destinations and amenities are most popular with the target demographic. He also had Carlos run AI-powered sentiment analysis on the user reviews to better understand the emotional tone connected to the most popular rentals.

Ethan used this collection of information, along with other social media data the hotel purchased, to create a demo. The demo showed a young family using the AI-powered mobile application to book a customized suite equipped with amenities such as laundry service, Instacart delivery of diapers and the kids' favorite snacks stocked in the room upon arrival, and customized TV channels suited for family viewing. The family was also given discount coupons for local child-friendly events like museums, parks, and zoos, which were sent to their hotel account on the mobile application. Ethan's and Carlos's concept fast-forwards through the years, and as the toddlers grow, it changes the recommendations.

The design team was waiting for Mei to gain clarity on the concept so they could get more deeply involved. And they were completely unaware of Ethan's project. In the meantime, they created research plans to test concepts before too much time had been invested. They knew from experience that the more product or engineering teams invested, the more attached they were to their work, regardless of customer feedback. If the design team didn't get customer feedback early enough in the process, they would be told, "We don't have time," which was shorthand for "I want to build my own idea, so I plowed past that step."

In summary, Barry and Mei were working on what they thought would make Carol happy. Ethan was moving on his ideas, based on what he thought would make an impressive technical demo, and the design team was preparing to get involved when given the go-ahead.

One day, Carol scheduled an update meeting with all the leads. Each was working with their own executive team and had not gotten together to discuss one single direction. Mei went first, and Carol liked the concept. (Interestingly, Carol did not ask if customers liked the concept.) Carlos was up next. Carol stopped him after two minutes to ask why his technical demo had nothing to do with Mei's presentation. She asked the executives why they were telling different stories. Ethan literally pointed to Carlos and said, "I thought you were working with Mei, but I guess not." No one believed him, because everyone knew Ethan had more power than anyone, including Carol. If he liked his own idea, that's what would be built.

The cultural norm in this department was the higher up the problem starts, the less people are willing to speak up. This kept the design team from asking Mei to get alignment with her peers or escalate to Melanie that they were struggling to get involved. This same culture allowed Ethan to imply Carlos hadn't done his job. Finally, this culture kept a team of fifteen or so people silent in the face of Ethan's unfair characterization of Carlos, even though Ethan had a reputation for bullying, and Carlos had a reputation for being one of the greatest guys you could have on your team.

The mere act of creating a So That template would have pulled everyone together to come to agreement on customer and business outcomes. This would have revealed Ethan's early investment in a demo, as well as the lack of coordination between his team and Barry's. At this point, they would have had several options to create alignment. They could send their teams off to discuss and come back with ideas that represent the best of what the teams have to offer. They could have involved the designers and conducted user research to give them a concrete direction. Whatever they chose to do, they would have been much more likely to act as one team working together to solve the same problem. The team would have saved weeks of time and preserved the psychological safety of the team.

Overbooked: An Opportunity-Based Outcome

Let's look at a time when the So That method was used to identify a new business opportunity. These are the moments I live for! A simple fifteen-minute exercise can open a whole new way of looking at the business and unleash creativity, which results in employee engagement.

We're going to shift away from our squad for this example. Overbooking flights is a necessary reality in the airline industry. Every year, airlines spend thousands of dollars incentivizing passengers to voluntarily give up their seats on overbooked flights, often by offering financial compensation in return. There are even travel experts who help people make the most of this cash opportunity; some industrious passengers have created steady passive income streams by capitalizing on airline overbooking payments. Airlines track the overbooking compensation numbers and, of course, are always looking for ways to keep those numbers to a minimum.

I worked with an organization that carefully tracked this data point. The stated goal was to see "$0.00 in the spreadsheet" where financial compensation for overbookings was tracked. As a human-centered designer, I help organizations build their success by providing value to their customers. In this situation, the challenge amounted to removing a form of compensation the customer found valuable and replacing it with something that was financially better for the airline. I had been working with this organization for a couple of years and had the benefit of knowing that almost everyone who worked there was conscientious and cared deeply for their customers. I predicted the company would drop the idea the moment they realized the outcome was likely to frustrate their customer base.

To quickly get to that point, I started the So That process.

> We want to reduce the amount of money spent on compensating customers who give up their seats on overbooked flights so that we can reduce our costs.

Oops! Where was the customer? The So That method revealed a business outcome that was about cost reduction, not about value for people. I was stuck. The best possibility I could find was "so that we can reinvest those resources into something more valuable for the business and our customers." That's not an outcome. That's me trying to put a positive spin on my discovery.

Technically, we could say that cost reduction is the outcome of an action, but that's *business hygiene*, not a valuable customer outcome. The business should always be managing costs; don't take this situation out on your customers. Furthermore, a statement like "$0.00 in the spreadsheet" is difficult for a multidisciplinary team to connect to. Where is the motivation for people in that statement? Most people want to serve their business but not at the expense of their customers. This organization also had a powerhouse of innovative, creative people who deeply understood the business. I knew the executives wanted to engage their people's talents to improve the business, but they were starting from a place that would inhibit, rather than unleash, creativity and innovation. Look at the value this little So That exercise already provided.

Working together, the creatives and I shifted the conversation and put the customer at the center. We asked ourselves how we might bring value to the customer in ways that would reduce the potential for overbooked flights in the first place, which would reduce the need for financial compensation when customers were asked to surrender their seats. Taking this approach opened our minds to *opportunity-based outcomes*—outcomes that would grow the business by adding value for its customers.

We introduced a thought experiment: "What if the number in the spreadsheet stays the same, *but* we are able to introduce new value for customers whose consumption of this new value increases revenue equal to 10x the number we wanted to reduce?"

I remember posing that question to the executive leadership team and getting blank stares in return. They had been laser-focused on cost reduction, and what I was proposing was radically outside their organizational cost-reductive culture. Requirements flowed in a certain direction, and "change the number in the spreadsheet" was flowing down from the executives. Not that people were intentionally being obstinate or closed-minded. Their culture was blended with the processes they used to run their business and enmeshed with how they measured success, which in this case was by reducing costs in the spreadsheet. Working outside these parameters, especially without preparing people for doing so, meant potentially upsetting the applecart. As a consultant, I understood this: people in the room are left with the consequences of my actions. The most likely negative outcome was that my client would be unhappy if I didn't get them what they were asking for, and I would be reassigned (or worse).

I'm deeply committed to the So That method because it has served me so beautifully throughout my career. But what did I do when faced with a client who was hearing something they could not absorb? I forged forward with my methodology anyway! I knew from designing dozens of products and services for customers over the years that the heart of customer loyalty is the relationship. Let's create a great relationship between my client and their customer built on value! Honestly, in this situation, I couldn't go forward in good conscience doing anything else—it's just not who I am. I'd rather be reassigned or even change companies than be asked to work on a project knowing I would negatively impact the relationship between my client and their customer. One more thing to note is, since I was consulting, I needed to get the client an outcome they hadn't been able to get for themselves. It's a privilege that comes with consulting, but it comes at a high price if I miscalculate. Hence my method, which forces me to think through exactly which outcome is right and how I'm going to get that outcome.

After my suggestion regarding how to look at the problem was rejected, I asked everyone but the cross-functional doers of the team (designers, developers, and product owners) to leave the room so we could work on our proposal. We explored ways to add value, even if the number in the spreadsheet never changed. I was curious to see what the team would come up with. These were clever people, and they knew their customers very well. It wasn't long before they were riffing off each other. Ideas were flying around the room; people were sketching, sharing scenarios, and combining them to create new things. The team's energy was palpable.

I am not at liberty to share the final solution we landed on, but over the course of an afternoon, we created a brand-new idea. Knowing we were going to present a radical approach to the executives, I wanted to ease them into the concept in a way that gave them a sense of choice instead of all-or-nothing. If they felt it was all-or-nothing, they would likely choose nothing because they didn't have the culture, leadership, or organizational structure in place to proceed with a whole new kit and caboodle.

I had the team package up the idea as a series of experiments that demonstrated incrementally adding value for their customers, while learning along the way. We also presented a series of suggestions for reducing the customer pain of being removed from a flight. This added value to the customer by reducing their level of inconvenience and added value for the airline staff by reducing the potential for someone at the gate to demand as much money as possible. The team worked out who would pitch which part of the idea, and we rehearsed a few times.

The heart of customer loyalty is the relationship

A few days later, the executives returned. I gave a brief introduction of the collaborative design process our cross-functional team followed and explained how the different disciplines brought their experience and knowledge to the table to arrive at what they were about to see through co-creation. Then the team took the lead, and I parked myself in a corner of the room and listened.

The executive team was absolutely thrilled with the innovative direction! They were impressed with how the team blended their subject matter expertise seamlessly to arrive at an outcome that enhanced both the customer value and the business outcomes. The team was committed to their ideas. Even as they rotated through the different portions of the presentation, they functioned as one unit, amplifying each other's messages and calling out the value their partnership brought to the work.

By the time we finished a week of workshopping, idea generating, and presenting, the team shared a vision they were excited to deliver. The executive leadership paved the way for the experiments to commence, and relieved, I got on a plane back home to San Francisco. This was possible, in large part, because all the outcomes were so clear. It was easy for everyone to get aligned on the business outcomes, which emerged directly from the customer outcomes. The team could see how they were adding value for customers, and that gave them purpose.

I'm thrilled to say that a couple years after this experience, I read about my former client's success in the press as they rolled out their experiments. They were doing first-of-a-kind work, differentiating themselves from their competitors and shifting the industry by adding customer value.

Connecting Outcomes to People

A well-formed business outcome clearly communicates its value. When you have alignment between the outcome's value and the people who work to create the outcome, the people are more likely to be inspired and give their best. Alignment toward outcomes shifts culture from platitudes on posters in the hallway to a deep sense of employee engagement to accomplish something meaningful. And it makes it unmistakable when people are acting at cross-purposes, so they can shift to more synergistic ways of working.

A few pages earlier, we saw the chaos Always Home's innovation software squad experienced under leadership that was not aligned on outcomes. Ethan and Barry independently tried to figure out what they thought would bring back their target customers. This guesswork introduced a level of risk into the equation. What was at risk? Wasted time, energy, and talent, ultimately exhausting the team and impacting morale. Contrast that with the airline that kicked off a project with clear outcomes for their customers and rallied the whole team to deliver that value.

If culture is the expression of what an organization values, we want the team's motivation and engagement right at the top of the list. When the people in an organization are aligned with outcomes and their impact on customer value is clear, it's easier to engage. For example, I've interviewed hundreds of designers and never once when asked what motivates them did they say, "Making money for my employer." People usually go into design because they want to make the world a better place for their customers. Designers are not unique in this. We feed this motivation when business outcomes are built on customer value, and that connection is obvious to every employee.

A culture built for outcomes means people *desire* to believe in and align with the business outcomes, and thus they are more likely to share values, beliefs, and the necessary behavioral norms. When outcomes have an inherent and clear value, it's easier for people to align and contribute to the execution of those outcomes. Outcomes that create a cycle of value for the business foster continued engagement.

3

The Human Factor

In the social jungle of human existence, there is no feeling of being alive without a sense of identity.
ERIK ERIKSON

HUMAN BEINGS are essential to any business. Technology can optimize, automate, and show us connections no human mind would be able to find on its own, but the human beings that come to work every day are the creative power behind business innovation and success. Human beings provide, above all, judgment. There are people in your organization who understand how you got where you are today, who the collective "you" wants to be three years from now, and who will forge a pathway to that new reality if they believe in it. People understand the nuance of orchestrating the technical and nontechnical across groups to deliver outcomes for other people. Therefore, we need to make sure people have the culture they need to drive business outcomes.

Why, then, don't business leaders spend as much effort on developing culture as they do on adopting and educating their teams about new technology and honing business processes? I believe most business leaders erroneously think they do.

Many companies communicate culture through statements and perks intended to indicate they value people. By now, we know company culture is not a foosball table or beer bash Fridays. And we also know it's not a twenty-five-page HR policy or a rambling string of late-night CEO tweets. Valued people thrive, right? Well, there's more.

Addressing the human being requires understanding how people think, make decisions, respond to their environments, and learn new things, to name a few. It's part psychology, part neuroscience, part anthropology, and for those of us in technology, it's also part technology. Add in some sociology and physiology, and you've got a good start.

"Human factors" is a term that refers to the application of the understanding of human psychology and physiology to the design and engineering of processes, organizations, material objects (called industrial design), and/or software products. The goal of considering human factors is to enhance user experience and outcomes and to eliminate pain, frustration, and injury.

My field, human-computer interaction, is one discipline within human factors. I've worked at the intersection of human beings and technology, looking at physical and cognitive abilities and limitations of human beings, as well as how the physical environment impacts them and their use of technology. All these elements factor into how I help people get great outcomes. My goal has always been to help the companies I work for make their technology extremely valuable to the user and seamlessly weave it into the worlds of human beings, so the outcomes feel natural.

The Role of Identity

Most people have a professional identity. In their 2014 article, "Forming and Developing Your Professional Identity: Easy as PI," in *Health Promotion Practice,* Heather Honoré Goltz and Matthew Lee Smith define professional identity as "critical to a person's sense of self: It is about connecting with roles, responsibilities, values, and ethical standards unique to a specific profession." This is different from your core or personal identity—the sense of who you truly are—that developed due to the influence of family, friends, community, genetics, experiences, race, sex, and so on.

For many people, professional and personal identity are tightly woven together, which is not a bad thing; it's just something to be aware of. Throughout this book, I will draw your awareness to the role of identity in relationship to different kinds of friction that emerge when there is a mismatch of culture and outcomes. For this reason, pay close attention to how deeply intertwined your personal values and identity are with your professional identity.

Consulting is an area where my personal and professional identities are intertwined. I've always felt personally responsible for anything I create. The sense of personal accomplishment is a strong motivation for me. As a consultant, I felt a special connection to my clients. (If you have worked with me, know that I'm thinking about our time together as I write this book.) Though I was acting on behalf of a larger company, the connections I felt with my clients were personal, and my sense of responsibility toward them was deep. They were personally trusting me with their business results. This led me to take personal and professional risks I did not take as a software designer (as I shared in the story about airline overbooking) to get my clients the outcomes they deserved.

I don't regret any of those risks; they all paid off. But personally, I paid a higher price than was necessary because I didn't see how deeply my professional and personal identities were enmeshed. I wouldn't separate these identities because I like the motivation and sense of accomplishment. Yet had I the awareness earlier in my career, I would have made different choices. Pay attention to where your identities and values intertwine so you can both make choices that are in alignment with your intentions and not force colleagues in directions that are designed to support your personal needs.

Ripples of Change

While designing enterprise software for Fortune 1000 companies, I leaned into innovation. I'm happiest on the bleeding edge of advancing businesses. It is very important to solve existing problems, and yet problem-solving doesn't grow businesses as much as finding new opportunities to differentiate yourself and staying a step ahead of the competition.

As I tested concepts with users, I observed a pattern of ambivalence. In this context, the term "user" refers to the person actually using the software, versus the customer, which in this example would be the company that purchased the software. It would take convincing the user, and often working up the management chain on their behalf, to try these opportunity-generating innovations for any length of time. Although users raved about many of the concepts they were testing, they weren't jumping in, and it turns out the problems were human and organizational.

For example, in the early 2000s, I was designing software that helped developers investigate the guts of their applications to see how they were working. Imagine you're on your bank's website transferring money. You click the Transfer button and get the spinning icon that tells you the website is executing your request. It spins... And it spins... It seems like the website isn't responding. You need to know the status of your transaction, so you call the bank. They look on their end, tell you the transaction went through, and direct you to refresh your page. The page updates, and what you see matches what the customer service representative told you. All is well and you go on with your day.

Now, imagine the customer service representative receives ten calls describing the same problem in a three-hour period, which is very unusual. He opens a ticket with the operations team that monitors all the applications on the banking website. The level one operator runs some diagnostics and finds that Bill_Pay transactions are running slower than normal and a higher percentage of them are timing out. Here's where the software I designed would come in. In a nutshell, the software would visualize for the operations team how everything inside the Bill_Pay application was running. Applications are made up of lots of little events. In this example, the Bill_Pay application might, among other things:

- Authenticate the user
- Go to database A and get their account totals to show the available funds
- Render the page with all the user's existing payees
- If the user adds a new payee, go to database B to see if the bank already has this payee in the system or needs to add it; if need be, gather new payee information and send it back to database B

- After the bills are paid, store the bill totals back in database A, so the user can see a record of all their bill payment transactions

Applications talk to each other, to databases, and to many other things. It's helpful to be able to see if a problem is happening inside an application or in a call out to another part of the system. For example, maybe the database is not responding.

Back in the early 2000s, this was groundbreaking. (Today it's in all troubleshooting software.) The ability to look at exactly how an application was functioning seemed miraculous to users. When I showed these concepts to customers, they were thrilled to be able to identify a problem inside an application or rule out the application as not contributing to the problem, all in a matter of minutes. This could literally take days off the troubleshooting. When I asked the operations teams at various companies who would use this tool, I expected to hear a level one, level two, or level three operator. Imagine my surprise when the answer was consistently "We don't know."

We had something incredibly useful that my customers wanted, but they didn't know who would use it or where it would fit in their process. The concept was both exciting and too disruptive to adopt.

Everyone had roles that mapped to outcomes they were supposed to achieve. To achieve these outcomes, they worked either independently or as teams. Adopting this technology would:

- Require changing the process some people used

- Temporarily slow down the team as they learned the new process

- Shift roles, which introduced the potential for misalignment between the new value they are expected to provide with the software and the value they had been expected to provide

- Introduce the potential for missed target goals as the team learns new software, adjusts roles and processes

It was too much to expect the team to do their day job *and* all of the above at the same time, at least not without a clear road map. These kinds of changes need to be planned and staged, and that takes time and effort. These changes cause different kinds of friction for people (and we'll go deep into that in the next chapter). For now, we want to be mindful that human beings have cognitive and psychological reactions to change that may not seem like direct responses to those changes. In fact, for many of my software clients over the years, the idea of change alone was enough to make them resist adopting new technology. The people I worked with seemed to perform a gut cost-benefit analysis on the fly, resulting in a "no, thank you" rejection of the technology.

More digging taught me the rejection wasn't because the software lacked value. When asked what people would add or how they would change it, there was little constructive feedback. The problem wasn't the software; the problem was I wasn't talking to agents of change. I was talking to operators who were tasked to get specific outcomes. Even though we could calculate projections of better outcomes *with* the new software features, none of these people knew how to enact systemic change. They monitored infrastructure and applications for a living. If I could have flipped a switch and put them into a new world where the processes, roles, identities, and so forth were ironed out and everyone was working in a steady state, they would have taken the software on the spot.

The moral of this story is that change ripples throughout organizations. Users struggled to adopt new game-changing software because its impact would ripple out beyond their spans of control. Along with the software, I needed to understand and support the bigger human impact this software created. I needed to provide a new vision of their organization and its outcomes, as well as a pathway of getting from today to tomorrow. It's so obvious now, but people cannot go somewhere if they don't know where that somewhere is! There's a great quote attributed to Yogi Berra: "If you don't know where you are going, you might wind up someplace else."

Visibility for You

People need to see where they fit into the outcome and how, so they can be assured of their value. Without this initial validation, a big shift can feel very risky, and people worry about their futures.

In her book *The Willpower Instinct*, Kelly McGonigal, PhD, a professor at Stanford University, writes about brain imaging studies showing that when we think of ourselves in the future, we use the same region of the brain used for thinking about *other* people. We see our future selves as separate entities from ourselves in the current moment.

Isn't that fascinating? To you, the future you is someone else! You haven't become that person... yet! However, the more clearly your role and its outcomes are defined, the easier it is for you to develop a pathway to your future self. We can't jump into a future professional identity, however small the changes are from today, without knowing where we're going. This doesn't need to be a big deal, but it will become a big deal if this work isn't done.

It's hard for human beings to move toward a destination they cannot imagine when they do not feel a personal connection. In the previous section, I was introducing new technology to my users that changed how they saw themselves. That future self was not how they identified themselves in the moment—it was another person. We solved this problem by bringing users into the design and development processes. They helped us understand how the technology was impacting them as people, meaning how they made decisions and how they worked with their peers. We then used that information to keep these impacts minimal and to help users along the way. We also made sure to include support for these changes in the sales cycle. (Tech readers, this is one of the reasons people don't use your software. You've made your software more valuable than a competitor's, but you haven't made the value of your software worth the *price of the change* that needs to take place to use a new product or replace an existing one.)

Change impacts people in ways you don't expect. Change impacts how someone sees themselves, as well as how they connect to and work with those around them. If you expect this and make room for it, people have a much easier time adopting change, and you avoid some of the friction we talk about in Chapter 4. To explore the impact of change on identities, check out the empathy map and hopes and fears exercises found in the back of the book.

Your Brain on Threat

When I moved into consulting, I experienced even more acutely what happens to people as they move through big changes that impact one's personal or professional identity, or their ability to predictably deliver value. To better understand why people respond the way they do, let's consider a little anatomy.

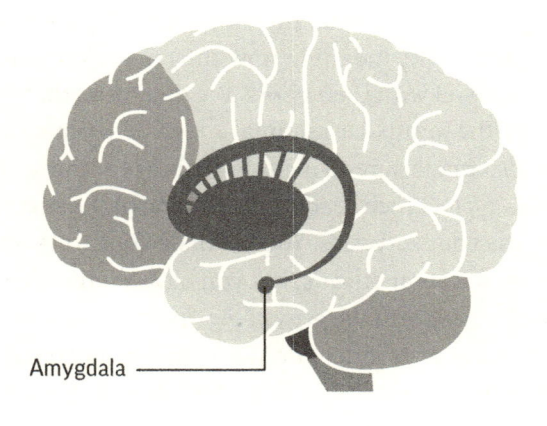

Amygdala

Stimuli comes in through our senses: smell, touch, taste, sight, and sound. When the stimuli are perceived as threatening, a region in the brain called the amygdala is activated. The amygdala sends out signals to prepare the body for the threat, initiating a fight, flight, or freeze (or sometimes fawn) response. These signals are passed between the brain and the rest of the body through the nervous system, which regulates, well, just about everything. To quote the Cleveland Clinic's website, "Your nervous system keeps track of what's going on inside and outside of your body and decides how to respond to any situation you're in."

What then is a threat? The answer depends on who you are. For most people, a charging bear would set the amygdala screaming out orders. You might freeze, you might run, you might be a well-prepared hunter and use weapons and bear spray to protect yourself. All three of these responses include some level of arousal: dilated pupils, blood pulling back from the digestive system, increased heart rate, rapid breathing, and reduced activity in the prefrontal cortex.

Interestingly, the prefrontal cortex "intelligently regulates our thoughts, actions and emotions through extensive connections with other brain regions," according to the Yale University School of Medicine. Neuroscientist Matthew Lieberman found an inverse relationship between amygdala and prefrontal cortical activity. When the amygdala lights up under threat, the prefrontal cortex dials down, reducing our ability to think. In Alla Weinberg's book, *A Culture of Safety*, she notes that under threat, our IQ can drop to as low as 50 to 70 points. For context, the average IQ is 100. This means when people feel threatened, they are half as intelligent as the day you hired them. (This fact alone should be enough to spark intentional culture design!)

Swap the threat of a charging bear for being undermined in front of your executive leadership. And in a post-pandemic world, that public embarrassment is probably recorded on Zoom, no less.

Whew! Just thinking about that elevates my breathing and heart rate. Mentally and emotionally, I'm sent back to any number of memories of coaching teams and their leadership out of similar situations. When something is perceived as a threat, it triggers the mind and body to seek safety, and the nervous system moves into survival mode.

There's only one nervous system, not one attuned to life-or-death threats and one to irritating work situations. A threat is a threat. Yet we expect our nervous systems to distinguish and respond only to *real* threats to our physical safety. You probably work because you must. It puts a roof over your head, provides medical care, food, education—things needed for *survival*. Discord at work is a very real threat for many and, in my opinion, rightly excites the amygdala.

In his 1999 book, *The Developing Mind*, Daniel J. Siegel described the "window of tolerance," which represents your comfortable range of emotional experiences. When operating inside the window, you can easily cope with the level of stress you are experiencing. When the level of stress goes outside the window, you move into hypo-arousal or hyperarousal, depending on your personal response to that specific stressor.

When you slip into hyperarousal, your anxiety escalates, you feel agitated, and you may feel compelled to act in ways like raising your voice or having an outburst. When you have the other reaction, hypo-arousal, you start shutting down. You may feel numb, zoned out, unmotivated, depressed, and even very sleepy. These are signals that you feel powerless; your amygdala has told your body it's time to withdraw. It's important to recognize these symptoms. Windows of tolerance are unique to each person. Being aware of what sends you into hypo- or hyperarousal can give you back some control.

Remember our software squad from the hotel? There were a few people on the squad's leadership team who were regularly overwhelmed by the stress of the project. They operated on the edge of their window of tolerance on a regular basis,

HYPERAROUSAL
- Overreactive, unclear thoughts, emotionally distressed

CAN'T CALM DOWN

WINDOW OF TOLERANCE
- The body is in its optimal state
- Can access both reason and emotion, mentally engaged

SHUTTING DOWN

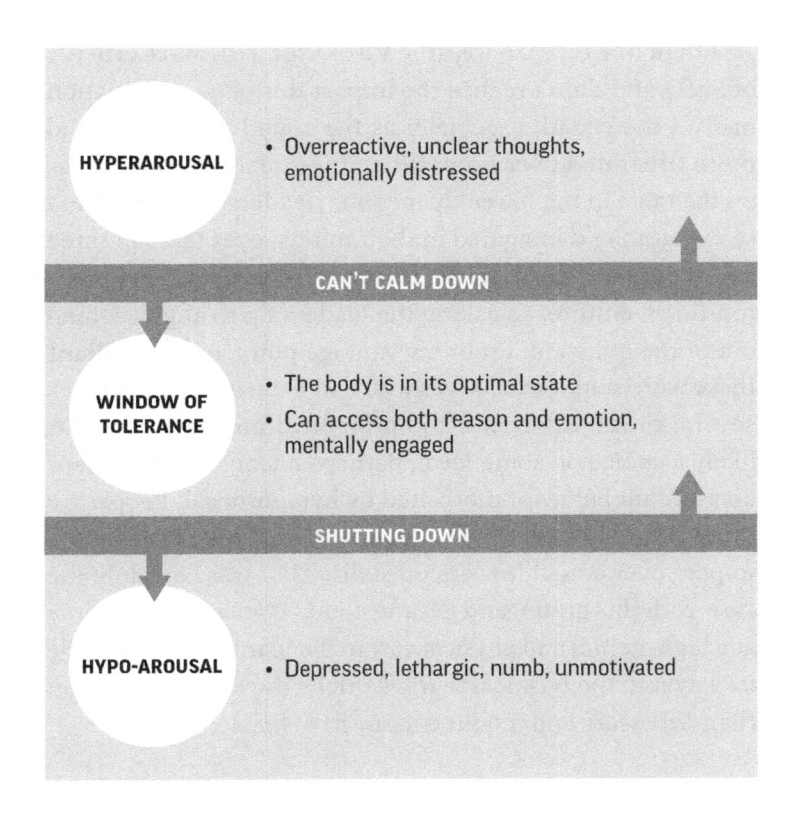

HYPO-AROUSAL
- Depressed, lethargic, numb, unmotivated

spitting out thinly veiled insults like lead shot when they slipped over the edge into hyperarousal. The squad knew this. Everyone in the innovation center knew this. When pressure got high and the threat of potential outbursts increased, the rank and file crept over to hypo-arousal and withdrew. This cycle is common and leaves stores of human potential untapped because people are too stressed out to function at a high level. Understanding how threat impacts our ability to think and work, we can see how this situation wore the team down emotionally and cognitively.

Ethan (the CTO), Barry (the VP of Product), and Carol (VP of Software) didn't realize the impact this ongoing situation had on the squad, especially as the squad grew more and more frustrated over time. When the squad put their ideas on the table in the biweekly meeting, leadership often didn't see what they'd imagined in their minds' eyes (and all three saw different things), so they criticized the work. This was a top-down culture, so asking the leadership to align seemed out of the question. From my vantage point as a consultant, these were senior executives who had been around the block several times. Advanced and prolonged misalignment was likely a choice on some level, perhaps unconscious, perhaps an avoidant behavior motivated by hypo-arousal. People are often promoted because of technical expertise or business impact over actual leadership skills. That was certainly the case with this group, and getting good business results came at a high mental and physical cost to the team. This cost made its way into the business; early work by the team took longer than necessary and required many fixes for sloppy work.

The Bear in the Boardroom
I'd like to share a personal story about the threatened brain from my own work experience. I started my career in technology in the late 1990s. There were very few women in traditional technology companies; they were especially rare in product development organizations and even rarer in designer roles. As a woman who was not accustomed to working with all men, I had a hard time being heard. Because the discipline of design had yet to be fully recognized for its business contributions, I had a hard time getting into the right conversations. I was talked over in meetings, other people took credit for my ideas, my hard work was dismissed, and I spent a lot of

my late twenties and early thirties feeling incensed at work. I had to learn to communicate in ways that were not organic to who I was. At that time, people didn't understand the role of human factors and didn't consider the whole person in a work setting.

Fast-forward a decade. The world had changed to the degree that my earlier struggles faded into the background, and my contributions as a designer were valued. I started a new job, but unbeknownst to me, there was a real character in my organization. Rudy was a bear. His language reminded me of what work had felt like ten years prior. He was intentionally divisive, unnecessarily provocative, and sometimes just plain insulting.

Early in my tenure, we were in a meeting with five or six other people. I was mid-sentence, sharing some user feedback we'd received and discussing the changes we needed to roll into the next release when Rudy's voice arced over the whole conference room table. Before I'd even made my point, Rudy had decided how the team was going to address the feedback (which he hadn't heard in its entirety), and it was time to move on. I lost my mind—on the inside. Rudy was an executive, and I was not. My presence and my six weeks of research and synthesis had been completely dismissed with one hot bellow. I went silent and numb (hypo-arousal).

I looked around the room at my colleagues, all men, and no one batted an eye. A few minutes later, Rudy did the same thing to James, a technical architect who was not an executive. James raised his voice over Rudy's and continued. I braced for the war that was about to break out. The others sat there like they were watching snowy plovers run along the water's edge. We were having two different experiences. Mine was informed by my previous challenges at work, my sex, age, and personal

We take our whole selves to work

---

history. These men were informed by their own experiences. Who knows, perhaps they were all dying inside, too, but it didn't seem like it. James did not appear bothered in the least.

I don't know what was happening for my colleagues, and they didn't know what was going on for me. When we left the room, they went back to their desks, and I went out for a walk. I got a coffee, found a bench at the Ferry Plaza, and called a friend. I expressed to her my outrage, how angry I was because I was talked over *again*... My work dismissed *again*... I felt invisible *again*... To continue with this team, I had to reduce face time with Rudy, build a web of support for my data and designs before showing them to him, and sometimes skip soliciting his feedback altogether. From Rudy's perspective, this probably looked like disengagement. From my perspective, I had fallen out of my window of tolerance, and I was doing what I needed to do to remain productive. Eventually, I was transferred to a different department, and things got much better.

The point is we take our whole selves to work. We may think we're operating 100 percent above the board, but we are all being influenced by our life experiences and our neural circuitry, which makes decisions without consulting our consciousness. To be clear, I'm not advocating for meetings to turn into therapy sessions. There is ample evidence to suggest we pay attention to the signals and to investigate why people behave the way they do. When people act out or don't perform as well as expected, it's very often due to a perceived threat or a lack of information, like several of the misalignments and lack of outcomes at Always Home. There is some kind of friction in the human system, and people are triggered into a level of stress outside their window of tolerance. Clarity and transparency of intention, outcomes, and what change means for your identity and the identities of those around you can improve and sometimes even eliminate the stress response.

Human factors, or understanding human psychology and physiology, are critical to understanding how to create an environment that allows teams to function at a high level and achieve desired outcomes. Knowing what makes people tick, and what triggers slowdown, is part of intentional culture design.

4

The Invisible Maze

The psychological rule says that when an inner situation is not made conscious, it happens outside, as fate.
CARL JUNG

IN THE EARLY 2000s, I worked in a startup. At the beginning, we were growing by leaps and bounds; it seemed every few weeks there was a new big change. One of these changes was hiring a director of product, Peg. Her role was to grow our product portfolio and improve operational efficiency by bringing in a consistent, repeatable practice to our Wild West mentality.

Peg wanted to instill a culture based on valuing people's time, which meant she did not want to participate in inefficient meetings that ran over schedule and often ended without insights or actions. Peg believed in only having meetings when there was a good reason for everyone to gather, when the meeting's outcomes were clear, and when everyone was prepared. If a meeting invite did not have an agenda and an outcome, Peg did not attend. There was just one problem: Peg *did not tell anyone* about the culture she was trying to instill, the values she thought should drive the culture, and the behaviors she expected to manifest.

Time and again, after waiting ten or fifteen minutes, people walked into Peg's office and asked if she was going to join the meeting. She asked about the agenda and the outcomes, and if there were none, she simply said, "No." Sometimes, someone would figure out an agenda and outcomes on the spot, and then Peg would go to the meeting. After several weeks, we figured out what it took to get Peg to a meeting, and we dutifully sent more thoughtfully prepared invites. But in the meantime, we resented being ignored by a key leader. Some people misunderstood Peg's signal and decided to skip meetings too. If she didn't care about the meetings, why should they? We did our fair share of grumbling about Peg behind her back because she allowed us to waste our time when she knew exactly what she wanted. She could have sat the team down and been clear about her expectations. Instead she decided to let us feel our way through the dark.

Let's be honest. Peg made an odd decision that puzzles me to this day, but it's not the worst thing I've seen—not by a long shot. Hired to bring order to our chaos, she created an atmosphere of tumult and fear. Until we figured Peg out, she felt unpredictable, which triggered feelings of threat. Once we understood what she was trying to communicate to us, she seemed manipulative and passive aggressive, further cementing people's feelings of threat.

As the boss, Peg had power over the individuals on the team. She also set the tone for acceptable behavior. Believing that Peg didn't care about meetings and using her own choices as examples (and a bit out of spite), people skipped meetings too. Communication waned, and after several months, the organization had not achieved the efficiency and productivity that Peg's VP expected when he hired her. Peg got some coaching and did a good job making changes to her leadership style. However, we never repaired the damage that had been done, which limited the team's success. The mistrust Peg caused, especially right out of the gate and with no other context of her, introduced friction that held the team back, even after the offending behavior ended.

Catalysts of Friction

New leadership and poor communication are just two examples of the many catalysts that introduce friction. Literally anything that impacts how individuals, teams, and organizations think about themselves and their work can introduce friction as well as culture change. Some examples are the rate of change, reorganizations, merging of product portfolios, mergers and acquisitions of companies, changes in leadership, restructuring of business processes, and economic factors.

In fact, friction is likely all around you, in big and small ways. Have you ever had the same meeting multiple times with no change in procedure or outcomes? Have two different leaders expressed a desire for two different courses of action when you thought they were driving toward the same goal (as Ethan, Barry, and Carol did)? Does your team struggle to produce results due to inefficiencies or a lack of coordination? Do you recall initiatives that were introduced as the new top priority only to see them fade away for no reason? These are all evidence of friction, and in each situation, there are one or more forces impeding alignment and execution.

When the needs of the whole human being are not addressed during prolonged challenges, three types of friction may arise: cognitive, psychological, and/or cultural. These friction points slow down progress, communication, alignment, and create a lack of trust that negatively impact business outcomes. I call this "the invisible maze." The invisible maze forms over time, as people respond to living under continuous, low-grade threat. Deep inside, you sense you are up against a force you cannot see, and you feel for an easier route, even if it means a different outcome. Something is better than nothing.

Cognitive, psychological, and cultural frictions are similar in that they happen inside a person. We don't see them happening, but we see evidence of their effects. I've listed some examples of behaviors observed when cognitive, psychological, and/or cultural frictions are present. These behaviors are evidence you've been pushed outside your window of tolerance into either hypo- or hyperarousal.

- Procrastination (hypo-arousal)
- Doubling down on an old behavior (hyperarousal)
- Silence or not asking for help (hypo-arousal)
- Disengagement such as tardiness, leaving early, skipping meetings (hyperarousal or hypo-arousal, depending on the circumstance)
- Digging in heels or refusing to try (hypo-arousal)
- High walls that slow or block progress (hypo-arousal)
- Sabotaging or destabilizing behavior like backchanneling, gossiping, and creating mistrust among peers—or rank and file, if you're a leader (hyperarousal)
- Working solo in collaborative environments (e.g., when the team meets, one person arrives with a complete presentation, putting everyone else in the position of giving

feedback, rather than co-creating), not sharing files or information (hyperarousal or hypo-arousal, depending on the circumstance)

I've observed similar behaviors and responses to the three different types of friction, which is why I use the metaphor of a maze. The causes are not always obvious, but they can be identified, and the friction can be lessened or removed and avoided in the future. The solution lies in the kind of friction being experienced, as we'll see when we discuss each type. These friction points are all intertwined—pull on one and the others respond, usually in the same direction. Removing or reducing friction is done by making the implicit explicit. As the puzzle pieces become visible, people can move from inaction to action, from fear to calm, and the nervous system responds accordingly.

Cognitive Friction

Cognitive friction is a term appropriated from the discipline of interaction design. It refers to how cognition, or thought, slows down in the face of unexpected results or missing information. The user expected result 1 to happen and instead result 2 happened. When the unexpected occurs, users must slow down or stop what they're doing to figure out what went wrong. Then they need to figure out if result 1 is even possible, a task which can lead to avoidant behavior. The motivation switches from possibility to "why bother?" In the case of missing information, you simply cannot continue because you don't have what you need. Or you choose to continue in whatever way you can, hoping you get near the goal. (For the record, this can be done well, with low risk, but that's usually an intentional choice to explore the information gap.)

Friction is likely all around you, in big and small ways

In the context of designing a culture for outcomes, cognitive friction happens when either the path forward or the outcome is unclear. When the team doesn't have what it needs, work slows down, and they turn to process in the hopes of speeding things up again. They don't realize the team has one or more *knowledge* gaps. These gaps usually occur in relation to organizational outcomes, or vision, purpose, and values. (More on these three driving forces in the next chapter.) From an operational point of view, cognitive friction can be very expensive in lost work, time, energy, and in good employees who decide to leave.

Let's revisit Always Home's software squad. Team morale was low due to how hard they had to work amid the churn of executive misalignment. The squad didn't stop working because of this. No, they worked even harder under the guidance of their respective leaders toward what amounted to a big question mark in the sky. Morale suffered because people felt their work would have no purpose until the executives were aligned and outcomes clear. Then the team could do its part to achieve those outcomes. This simple but profound gap affected a team of over a dozen people for months. Design, product ownership, and development were working next to each other toward slightly different goals, hoping they would magically intersect at some point. Multiply this situation by a larger team, or many teams within an organization, and we see how cognitive friction can introduce a cascade of amplifying inefficiencies throughout a system.

People may not even know they are experiencing cognitive friction. Has work ever just felt hard, as if you're accomplishing a lot of tasks, but you can't track forward momentum? Cognitive friction can halt progress as well. It may feel like you're swimming through a pool of Jell-O. There's no reward; it's just a slog.

Contrast this with digging into a problem in your field of expertise, and with clear outcomes. Even if the problem is hard, there's an energy and an excitement about the work that spurs you on. You feel connected to a sense of meaning. Every step provides some kind of value: what works, what doesn't, and why. A continual cycle of reward is coupled with a sense of accomplishment throughout the process.

Psychological Friction

Cognitive friction interrupts your ability to accomplish work with reasonable effort. It feels like part of the equation is missing—you need to take a class, hire a consultant, rethink a process. Psychological friction impacts you on a deeper level. It leads you to question your personal or professional identity and how (or if) you are in the right job or organization. With psychological friction, you feel you are not necessarily the source of the problem but definitely part of the equation. You feel that whatever catalyst for change is occurring, it must relate in some way to your identity, values, belief system, or something else very close to what makes you who you are. This may not be a conscious thought, by the way. But it triggers your nervous system, because it says to the brain, "You do not belong here" or "Someone with more power than you thinks you don't belong here."

One tricky thing about psychological friction is that we never really know what response it creates for another person. Your individual psychological state—your physical feelings, emotions, and thoughts—is developed over a lifetime, it is unique to you, and it will continue to evolve over time. It makes sense that what feels like a threat to one person does not trigger threat in another. (Think back to my reaction to Rudy versus the rest of the team's.)

To illustrate how psychological friction can impact a team and its productivity, let's turn again to our software squad. Jeffrey, the senior designer, works with Mei from the product team and with Carlos, the engineering architect. The three have worked together in the innovation center since its inception, about two years before our story began. They don't normally see software through to production; their work is customarily handed over to product teams. Once the project was decided on and the squad could collaborate, Carlos assumed the lead and started making decisions. Without including or consulting Mei or Jeffrey, Carlos prioritized work for the teams, made schedules, hosted stand-up meetings, and basically assumed a leadership role. Carlos came from a product team and had a deep knowledge of product lifecycle operations. He really was the best on the team to bring in technical processes, but not all the decisions. By taking on the role of leader without discussing it with the team, Carlos was also emphasizing the excessive power Ethan's organization had, which was an unintended consequence of what he thought was a gesture of goodwill. Because all three disciplines (design, product, and engineering) were working together on this application, every decision made by Carlos impacted Jeffrey and Mei.

From the outside, the project seemed to be running smoothly. On the inside, Jeffrey was experiencing psychological friction. He was responsible for the user experience. At previous companies he'd worked for, this was considered when developing and delivering applications. Because Carlos positioned himself as leader of the team meetings, he also positioned conversations about workflow from a mostly technical point of view. Carlos was not aware he was doing this; it was just his vantage point. In the meetings, Jeffrey regularly had to review Carlos's agenda and negotiate changes in how the team approached building the application to ensure all needs were met.

In short, Jeffrey felt steamrolled when Carlos took the lead. He was also afraid he would look petty if he challenged Carlos, especially because the project was finally going well. This meant Jeffrey had to work even harder to delicately undo Carlos's decisions without looking like he was trying to get his way. When Jeffrey approached Emma, the senior design manager, for some direction, she expressed disappointment that he needed this kind of help. Remember, Emma characteristically over-rotates and sounds like a dictator to her team. Her approach is to tell Carlos what's going to happen, but that is not Jeffrey's style, especially with a peer. Jeffrey is much more sensitive to the optics of things, to how people feel, and to building long-term relationships that serve the business. This is one reason why he was hoping Emma would be able to help turn this situation around.

Jeffrey was also experiencing psychological friction around his professional identity. Up until the situation with Carlos, Jeffrey had been an equal leader in this cross-functional team. Now he felt demoted, and he wasn't sure what his role was. Feeling his role had been undermined removed any sense of agency he felt he had to meet with Carlos to adapt the process. When Jeffrey reached out to his manager for support, he felt even more of a professional identity crisis, questioning if he had the right attributes and soft skills to do his job. Furthermore, he didn't feel he could discuss the problem with Emma.

Jeffrey was on the highest level of the design team; Jo and Arun took their signals from him. If Jeffrey wasn't challenging Carlos's leadership, they wouldn't either. The feeling of being second best, unable, and/or unqualified took over the team and created resentment. Emma's response to Jeffrey and the other designers, telling them, in essence, to just take what they need, made them feel psychologically unsafe because that wasn't how they worked with their peers. Furthermore, they didn't like how they felt when Emma did that to them. As they felt threatened by both Carlos and Emma, cognitive capabilities declined, and productivity slowed. Jeffrey was slipping into hypo-arousal. He was late to meetings, missed deadlines, and struggled to summon his creative powers to design during work hours. His most productive times shifted from collaborating with his teammates to working at night and on the weekends, when he was sure he would not encounter a critical voice.

If this wasn't disconcerting enough, because the design team was unfamiliar with the symptoms of friction, the leadership level of Melanie, Emma, Ethan, and Barry assumed the team just wasn't good enough for this project. The misdiagnosis made matters worse. On the bright side, we ran a series of workshops that drew out the actual friction points, allowing us to address the real problem and redesign as much friction as possible out of the system.

Cultural Friction

Cultural friction is caused by differences in values, belief systems, and the behavioral norms they drive. These can be team cultures or cultures of identity based on age, gender, nation of origin, or other factors. Cultural friction can profoundly impact individuals and teams. Everyone has belief systems and values that influence their perception of everything going on around them. Cultural friction can be described as the friction derived from the overall accumulation of differences in these perceptions when they are at odds. Cultural friction can cause psychological friction, but it differs in that the origin of the friction is one step removed from the individual. Cultural friction may (but does not always) cause a person to question their identity when belief systems clash. This topic can be a little murky, so let's parse out a few examples.

One person simply may not be a good fit for a strongly established team. This was true for me on Rudy the Bear's team: I was a terrible cultural fit! Aside from the psychological friction it caused me, I simply don't believe in raising one's voice at work, unless it's to shout "Hooray!" or "Great job!" My belief is that a voice raised in the context of strong negative emotions demonstrates a loss of control. In my belief system, repeatedly allowing oneself to lose control of one's emotions amounts to manipulation and bullying, and when that happens, it's time to pause. My colleagues appeared to be fine with Rudy's communication style. To get his attention, you had to become Rudy, and my brain just didn't work that way.

Unlike cultural friction due to a mismatch, differences in geographical or ethnic culture can cause a particularly intricate invisible maze of friction. In fact, cultural friction was the catalyst to psychological friction for Jo, the lead designer of the software squad. She lived in Beijing, and the Always Home headquarters was in San Francisco. As a remote employee at a Western company, Jo had to shift cultural contexts several times throughout the day when she took work calls at home. It was intuitive for her to blend back into her family and let go of work expectations when she was off the clock. Adapting to her Western work culture felt like using a mobile application to translate a conversation. She could adapt to some extent, but something felt unnatural. Jo was challenged by the soft skill and behavioral expectations.

Jo was told that as a lead, she needed to advocate more for her designs and for the design team, which meant she was expected to be more assertive with her cross-functional leaders. Jo had to really gear up to do this, and she often came on too strong or was perceived as argumentative or defensive because this behavior didn't come from a genuine place. Jo was experiencing cultural friction because her belief system did not yet align with her behavior at work. When Jo needed to act in a way that was inorganic to her, she forced it or skipped it altogether.

Jo and I worked through a few exercises to help identify her authentic leadership style. If her job expected her to pave the way for design, we wanted to find a way for her to do so while still feeling like herself. Alignment begins within. She knew she was capable of leading her team; she simply was not accustomed to the means by which leadership was executed at headquarters. After misfiring a few times to the higher-ups, Jo and I landed on a communication style that was effective for her, acceptable to her own leadership team, and well received by the people she led.

Understanding what's at play for human friction points is not straightforward, hence the metaphor of an invisible maze. The invisible part is that the friction is happening *inside* a person. The maze part is that internal friction is confusing. It's unsettling and uncomfortable. We know something is off, and even if we can't pinpoint what it is, it's there anyway, causing internal knots of discontent. Furthermore, people are most likely not consciously aware they are responding to invisible cognitive, psychological, or cultural friction. And they are likely even less aware if they are the ones causing it.

The Terrible Role Model

Take it from someone who knows. I (reluctantly) share a story of friction caused by (gulp) me. Yes, me and my own failures, but I believe in learning from mistakes, so please learn from mine.

I was in a leadership position in a worldwide organization. I had built and managed teams before and worked in start-ups, but this was the first time I had ever been on the ground floor of co-creating a business from scratch; employee number three, you might say. The culture was ours to mold. When people looked for signals about what behaviors, attitudes, and approaches were valued in the organization, they looked to me and the other leaders who had been there from the beginning.

Eighteen months into the organization's lifetime, the office was humming with people. It was lunchtime, and the team of fifteen was taking a break. They were sitting and eating together in a group, and one or two people were sitting nearby chatting on their phones. The overall vibe in the office was time to pause, reenergize, and connect with each other.

I was sitting in a corner working and eating my lunch. This was my practice every day. My role required that I regularly work sixty-five or more hours a week, and I was happy to do it. In fact, this was the happiest time in my professional career. I couldn't get enough of the work, the excitement, the growth. It was also challenging. There was so much to learn, so many people who needed my attention, and so many customers to work with.

Most days, I felt like I was in a pressure cooker. I was learning how to be a consultant, which entailed on-the-job training in front of clients. I was part of developing a worldwide design organization tasked with doing something none of us had done before—sit at the intersection of cloud adoption, digital transformation, and sales—and navigate a corporate political landscape I could barely identify, let alone understand. Then there were all the deals to be opened or closed, client relationships to be built. I absolutely loved this time in my career, but it was stressful. I looked forward to the evenings when the office emptied out. I stayed late and did the fun work of business design and creating the next thing to come. When I wasn't on a plane or in a hotel room preparing for client visits, I lived in that office, headphones on, dancing with my whiteboard and opening my mind to all the possibilities of the next set of outcomes we could offer customers.

On the day in question, while the team was enjoying their lunch break, I was approached in my corner by a senior developer named Heather. She asked if I had a few minutes to chat. "Of course!" I said, removing my headphones to give her my full attention.

She looked me square in the eye and said, "Sarah, you're a terrible role model."

I felt punched in the gut. I lost my appetite, and my face turned red-hot. I was flooded with a combination of feelings: grief, shame, anger, and helplessness. I was literally sitting in a corner, so I couldn't go anywhere. I briefly considered crawling under the table or running out the door but realized that would not turn things around. My internal defenses protested: *But I've poured my heart and soul into this new organization, cut me some slack!* This was the place where Heather and many more came to work every day. Now, here she was, telling me I was a horrible role model.

I took a deep breath and asked Heather to say more. At this moment, I was grateful for my training as a designer. I was able to detach from the emotion of the moment and take in her feedback with genuine curiosity.

My choices set the behavioral expectations for everyone around me

Heather shared what others saw regarding how I was showing up in the office, and it wasn't pretty. She said they saw me in a pressure cooker (true), working days, nights, weekends, and vacations (true). I never made time to sit with the team and have lunch (true). I never made time to engage with people on a personal level (true). And yet, Heather continued, I espoused "culture as the heartbeat of the organization" and prioritized this message when interviewing candidates for the organization (ugh, also true). Heather made it clear—and this was the most important thing I took away—that people looked to me to understand their place in the work community. In other words, they looked to me to understand their *professional identities*.

My behavior indicated, in many ways, that I did not uphold the values I raved about during team member interviews. Instead my behavior indicated that I valued the exact opposite. Heather helped me to understand the true messages my behaviors sent to the team.

- Sarah appears to be in demand 100 percent of the time. Team Interpretation: If I'm available to others, I must not be working hard enough or providing enough value.

- Sarah sacrifices personal commitments including family time, physical health, and emotional well-being. Team Interpretation: It appears that suffering for the sake of the job is valued over people with work-life balance and boundaries.

- Sarah bonds with other leaders over their sacrifices. Team Interpretation: She seems to thrive in a toxic culture and contributes to the wedge between leadership and those who aspire to leadership.

- Sarah's identity is of someone who creates opportunities for the business. Team Interpretation: Creating opportunities must be more important than the people who are fulfilling those opportunities.

See all the psychological and cognitive friction caused by my saying one thing and doing another? It's clear to me now, thanks to Heather, but at the time I was so utterly unaware of how my behaviors were being interpreted by the team, I was genuinely shocked when she brought the disconnect to my attention. I put people in the position of figuring out whether to align with their leadership or create another gravitational pull by aligning with each other.

Let's take a look at the impact of this friction on business outcomes.

The expected business outcome was customers who successfully modernized their enterprises through our expert methodology and technology. The team led customer engagements by partnering with the clients' employees to teach them our methodology and technology through immersive learning experiences. How well would our team perform if they were stressed out and exhausted or extending themselves every waking moment? The consequences to our business would be negative if the team was not 100 percent focused on their clients. That focus involved the delicate work of listening, observing, and teaching, all in the technical realm of writing software applications.

The team was the business—they had incredible talent to share. It was the responsibility of leadership to create conditions in which the team could be physically and emotionally healthy; to have the space they needed to take in what they were seeing on the front lines and bring it back into the business, so the business could evolve in concert with its customers. That co-evolution was a big part of our success, and it was dependent upon the team's wellness and awareness.

The level of friction my behavior created was devastating. It was the opposite of what the team needed. Yet my choices set the behavioral expectations for everyone around me. I made people feel uncomfortable taking breaks because I never took a break. People felt they were failing or falling short of expectations if they didn't exhibit the same behavior. I unwittingly increased cognitive load, brought about negative emotions, and made people question their identity and value in the organization. Terrible.

"Do as I say, not as I do" is poor leadership. To prevent such mistakes from continuing or happening again, I needed to examine what motivated my behavior. What was I getting out of it, and what did that say about my own values? Turning the mirror to look inward is not easy, but there was no way I could call myself a leader without doing so.

Being in demand 100 percent of the time made me feel like an important, valued part of the business. For most of my career, software designers were seen as optional. In this organization, my contributions were recognized at the highest levels of the company. Visibility brought adversaries from other areas of the company who either wanted what I had or felt encroached upon by the organization's success. I'd never had this kind of success before. Adversaries came with the territory, and I didn't recognize what was happening. Even if I had, I wasn't savvy enough to combat it properly. The only arrow I had in my quiver was to be in demand as much as possible. In my mind, being in demand equated to being essential, and I believed being essential made me safe in my role. That math doesn't work, as it turns out. Furthermore, it can hurt or misguide a lot of people.

Sacrificing personal commitments including family time, physical health, and emotional well-being was a continuation of the mind game I was playing. My sacrifices signaled to the company that it was my highest priority. In return, I was allowed to think of myself as "in," not just one of the rank and file but somehow special. It was as if each sacrifice was credit in some corporate account; the more I had in that account, the more protection I had and the closer I was to some inner circle of special people who were safe in their roles. (Thanks, amygdala!)

I didn't believe I would ever have this opportunity for success again, so I did everything I could to secure it. I was physically unwell, had lost over twenty pounds, and, against the direction of several doctors, maintained a nonstop global travel schedule. It wasn't until I was standing in the international terminal at San Francisco International Airport that I saw how foolish I was being. My sister, with whom I am extremely close, was in the emergency room with a heart issue. Her condition was out of the blue. When I'd gone to bed the night before, she was a healthy mother of two middle-schoolers and a wife. Now she was in the hospital with tachycardia as an emergency room team tried to get her heart rate under control.

I found a row of chairs by the ticketing counters and started to juggle phones. My sister was on my personal phone, texting me the details of her situation. On my work phone, I was texting my close work partner and co-leader to let her know I may not make the flight or the client engagement. Did you catch that? *May* not ... *C'mon*, Sarah!

My current-day self could just shake that woman in SFO, her Peet's coffee balanced on her little stack of Tumi carry-on luggage, texting on two phones at once. I wasn't critical path for this client engagement. I was trying to feel safe, trying to maintain the professional identity I had in the organization I helped build from the ground up, and clinging on to it over my own health and one of the most important relationships in my life. I had lost the plot.

(My sister is doing quite well now, and I am doing better too. My own health improvement is due in part to this reflection, so let's keep unpacking this Tumi carry-on of dirty laundry.)

Bonding with other leaders over our sacrifices was how I connected to my new tribe. I didn't set this tone, but I put on my floaties and jumped in! I was afraid that if I didn't engage, I would appear less dedicated than everyone else, despite my contributions to the business, recognition from every leader and client I'd worked with, and recognition from the top. Truth be told, the people underneath the leadership were rolling their eyes at us behind our backs, mocking our martyrdom. As I healed the motivations that drove my poor prioritization, I ran out of sacrifices—one healed the other. My connections with my peers also loosened, which was scary at the time, but I was headed in a different direction.

Identifying as someone who creates opportunities for the business at the expense of the fulfillment team was motivated again by my need to demonstrate, ad nauseam, my value. I worked All. The. Time.—trying to land the next big deal or develop a new competitive angle on the business. Multiple leaders in my organization told me to stop working so hard, but none could tell me why, other than that those around me who couldn't keep the same schedule felt bad. At the time, I didn't see that I was creating friction. This early in my consulting career, I lacked the confidence in my skills. I was doubling down (hyperarousal) on everything to try to calm my fears and project my professional identity.

I'd gone from one of the people responsible for creating a culture of safety, creativity, and innovation to an insecure person who couldn't differentiate her ideas from herself. The more recognition I received for my contributions, the more my ego got involved. I had profoundly conflated my personal and professional identities to the point that I felt the threat of annihilation if I wasn't actively progressing in a visible way. Some might sum that up in the term "workaholic," but we need to understand the values and motivations if we are to work our way out of toxic cultures.

The value reflected in my behavior was the need for safety, which I felt when I was part of the tribe of the leadership team. I was a co-founder of the organization, credited for much of its success, and I still felt like "just the designer." I had internalized the way I was treated by past colleagues: just the designer, optional, a pixel pusher. Couple that with my lack of experience as a consultant, and it's no wonder I felt so unsafe. It obscured my view, and I made some bad decisions.

We bring our entire selves everywhere we go. I bet you can think of a few people you've crossed paths with in your career who would do well with a little more self-awareness. And at times, maybe you can too. But there is an antidote! We can always step back and ask ourselves how our choices signal what we value.

Let's look at Heather, who did a wonderful job of demonstrating values that supported team health and growth and, by extension, the health of the business. She made an indelible mark on me the day she approached me with the truth for two reasons. The first was the information she shared. One single sentence changed my entire perception about where I fit in the organization and the power of my actions, and it set me on a course to make profound changes in my personal and professional lives. Second, Heather modeled for me true leadership by choosing to say something. Of course, I would have preferred she delivered the news a little more gently. Though if I'm being honest with myself, the starkness of her delivery, the surprise and sting of it, got my attention. Heather was not rude, but she also did not mince words. Her clarity was beautifully and organically Heather in nature.

Over time, the organization we worked for created additional leadership roles around the world, which both reduced the pressure on me and elevated more people into growth positions. We revamped our offerings, which allowed the organization to scale the work I was doing and the supporting knowledge across the organization. This added to the outcomes we could provide our clients, it expanded the team's knowledge of the business, and it impacted our bottom line. Oh, and it provided some recognition for my contributions! Frankly, the maze of friction I had created through my fear-driven knowledge hoarding and clamoring to feel valuable had been holding the organization back. Thanks to Heather, we were all able to get on a positive track and grow the business.

Whenever dealing with symptoms such as undesirable behavior, decreased quality of outcomes, poor performance, or operational inefficiencies, hunt around for areas of friction. If you're working with a colleague, remember to approach friction with curiosity and support. Most people will know what they need and can tell you if you make a safe place for them. Together you can go about making sure that friction can be addressed.

To remove friction from the system, we must attend to the critical intersection of culture, business outcomes, and leadership. Many pixels have been spilled on these three topics, their inextricable relationship, and how they fit together and influence each other. Friction happens in every organization, but knowing what to look for and what to do about it helps you move through it quickly and gets you and your team back to delivering great outcomes, while reducing the operational cost required to achieve them.

5

Designing Culture Change

Culture is not an initiative.
Culture is the enabler of all initiatives.
LARRY SENN

SEVERAL YEARS into my career as a consultant, I started noticing how influential culture was to my customers. Of course, I already knew how influential culture was from an internal standpoint. (I'd occasionally been a source of cultural friction and misalignment within my own organization after all.) But I began to understand how culture relates to my customers' ability to reach their outcomes (or not) when I was engaged in a research project on competitive consulting practices. I interviewed fifty technical consultants in various areas: security, artificial intelligence, blockchain, robotics and automation, and the like. None of the people I interviewed had human factors backgrounds, though some had more traditional outcomes-based consulting backgrounds. About two-thirds of them had been in their roles for many years and were considered experts in their fields. In the interviews, I asked them to brainstorm all the pain points they had experienced in the previous two years.

By far, the biggest pain point was they did not understand why customers did not do what they were told to do. This was stunning news. Several consultants said, "I gave them the presentation" or "I repeatedly explained to them how it works, and they just aren't doing it." The consultants were exasperated from running into invisible walls.

The importance of both culture and human factors were invisible to these consultants. They didn't see that professional identities needed to shift before people took different actions. They didn't see that disruption would occur whenever their clients intersected with people not part of these new initiatives, and the clients needed to be prepared to handle such situations. The organizations' values had to change so their clients could work productively toward new goals; it's the change in values, not rote memory, that triggers the awareness to take a different action. This kind of information—a shift in values—is not delivered the same way as intellectual knowledge. It cannot be memorized and played back at the right time.

An intellectual understanding of culture does not make it actionable because it hasn't permeated your belief system well enough to become a motivation that runs on autopilot; at this stage, culture is a thought experiment. For permeation to happen, you need to *experience* culture. Once you do that, you know if you feel aligned or if you can align to the values expressed by the culture. Values and purpose go hand in hand. Organizational alignment between its purpose and its values is what drives deep engagement. Alignment does not always happen. I've seen people change roles or companies because of differing values. These changes are always good. In follow-ups months and even years later, the people who made the changes are much happier working in cultures aligned with their values.

The Three Pillars of Cultural Alignment

There are three primary pillars in a culture for outcomes that together reduce or eliminate friction, create clarity, and inspire motivation. Those three pillars are vision, purpose, and values. We'll take a brief look at vision and purpose and then explore the vital role values play for aligning people to outcomes, regardless of the size of the team or the organization, and how integral they are for intentional cultural design.

1. Vision
Harvard Business School professor emeritus John Kotter defines vision as "a picture of the future with some implicit or explicit commentary on why people should strive to create that future." I chose this description because you need to be able to see a vision in your mind's eye. It's not an *idea* of the future; it's a *picture* of the future. By engaging, you are not achieving a metric, a sales quota to keep your job, or helping your team move the needle on every KPI; you are creating a future. Everyone should be able to visualize the outcomes and see themselves in the process. There's an exercise at the end of this book called a business impact worksheet that will help you start to sketch your vision. I encourage its use at every level of the organization to see how the vision flows throughout the teams. Everyone can identify their contribution and map it to the outcomes.

Equally important, Kotter requires that a vision include a reason for people to engage, a motivation for the human beings doing the work. There are two types of motivation:

- **Extrinsic motivation** is when your actions are motivated from outside rewards or punishments. These are things like trophies, awards, leaderboards, and other tools sometimes associated with gamification. I don't advocate for this type of motivation because it's often temporary and unsustainable. It can also create psychological friction. For example, if you're not getting your sense of accomplishment from your purpose, you will be at odds with yourself. Sure, you can do this for a bit, but the longer it goes on, the harder it will be to engage and do the job well.

- **Intrinsic motivation** is when your actions are motivated from the inside, from your own sense of gratification. Because it stems from your own desires, intrinsic motivation is a deeper driver; it sustains you through difficult times, and accomplishments feel more satisfying.

In a 2016 International Institute for Management Development article, authors Shlomo Ben-Hur and Nik Kinley write, regarding the missing piece in changing employee behavior, "It takes more than just knowing what behaviors must be altered to make [change] happen. Unless workers have the requisite abilities, inner resources (such as self-belief and resilience) and supportive work environments, it is difficult to make or sustain meaningful change."

The authors of an organization's vision are responsible for communicating why people should invest—why summon that intrinsic motivation? You need this to align yourself and others on the purpose and the outcomes of the work.

2. Purpose

Simply stated, purpose is the reason something is done. It is the "why." Purpose springs out of the vision and should encompass intrinsic motivation. Imagine an ocean wave headed toward the beach. The crest is the visible output, or the work that people do, while purpose is the invisible energy under the surface that propels the wave forward. When the vision is clear and includes a clear "why," people can more easily connect it to their own purpose, which sparks intrinsic motivation and creates engagement.

When building teams, I like to take this a level deeper and understand a person's purpose for their career path. I believe it's a key ingredient to the success I've had building teams. The very first thing I want to understand, even before someone's technical competence, is if they are a culture fit. To assess this, one of the first questions I ask candidates is "What makes you bound out of bed in the morning, and what makes you pull the blanket back over your head in dread?" The way a candidate answers this question provides insight into what motivates them. If it's extrinsic or doesn't seem motivated by helping people achieve outcomes, then they won't fit the culture of any organization I'm running. Hard skills cannot overcome a lack of intrinsic motivation and the drive created by a personal sense of purpose. When a department's or company's vision statement has a clear purpose that plugs into the purposes of the individuals on the team, you unleash incredible momentum and creativity.

3. Values

Values are the standards that represent right and wrong for the team, and they drive behavioral norms. Values are enduring core beliefs that are found in the ways people work, how they

It's the change in values, not rote memory, that triggers the awareness to take a different action

communicate, and the products they deliver. Values are ways of answering the question "What's important to this group?" You must be able to answer this question. If you cannot, you will either be unable to act with autonomy because you cannot discern the right answer, or you will create friction by making the wrong choice. We all make mistakes, but we don't want to introduce friction every day!

You also need the right conditions for people to feel motivated, to engage, and to thrive. You want to understand and feel attached to the organizational vision, see the purpose in the vision, and share the values. When you are aligned with all three pillars, you are acting in integrity with your conscience, evolving your skills and talent, and feeling deeply rewarded. (Hooray for intrinsic motivation!) In essence, people thrive when their belief systems and values are aligned with the work they are doing.

Actively aligning every individual with business values can feel daunting. I understand why an executive committee might be tempted to say, "We value collaboration, innovation, and work-life balance," throw a pool table into the breakroom, and then call it a day. "Off with you now—see you at your quarterly review!" It requires both business and human savvy, moving between human motivations and the work produced by those humans.

Vision, purpose, and values must be intentional, deliberate, and clearly connected to the business through people's day-to-day actions. We also need a plan to handle missteps. Human beings can suffer emotional damage through the words, actions, or even the lack of actions of others. We need to be prepared to reduce threats and promote psychological safety so individuals and teams can function at a high level.

Yet time and again over the last twenty-five years, I have encountered an undercurrent of chaos caused by business values that naturally conflict with the values of the people trying to work together. These conflicts arise because people are doing different jobs, are measured by different metrics, or define success in different ways. When jobs are different, the values and norms can be different. This adds friction to the system, but it doesn't have to.

We can think of these differences as eddies that either flow together, creating a powerful waterfall of acceleration toward business results, or class v rapids that overturn rafts, sending people swimming toward opposite shores for safety. Uncoordinated eddies leave it up to individuals and teams to figure out how to make meaningful connections with what they sense and observe the norms to be. This guesswork is risky and unnecessary.

Factor into this that few organizations properly define business outcomes, then fail to intentionally design the cultures needed to deliver on those outcomes. At best, this misalignment creates mild friction that prevents teams from reaching peak performance. At worst, confusion is introduced into the organization, affecting communication, quality, and operations, and disintegrating motivation. When intentionally designed to drive specific outcomes, culture connects human capabilities and wisdom with the business, and it drives choices in thought, action, and priority.

Mona Makes the Implicit Explicit

Let me tell you a story about a time I witnessed two teams functioning within a chaotic sea of mistrust that worked together to land on a safe shoreline; you might see yourself in one of these roles. I was working with an organization of senior directors who were trying to get their arms around digital transformation, what it could mean for their business, and how to get started. We had been workshopping for a day and a half. The vision was becoming clear. The people in the room were beginning to believe in the change they wanted to orchestrate across their organization. They were excited, and I was on top of the world!

The client was doing the very profound work of identifying their future selves and making incredible progress. Corporate transformation of this magnitude made living on airplanes and in hotels worth every bad meal, late flight, and lumpy pillow. Also, there was a contract worth tens of millions of dollars on the table, and there was pressure to build trust and get the client a vision they could use to springboard their transformation. But most importantly, this work gave them a solid foundation on which to build that transformation.

Standing in front of a wall full of a-day-and-a-half's worth of ideas written on stickies, we were coming down the homestretch when one of the directors, Mona, walked to the edge of the room and slumped down in a chair. This work is intense, so I wasn't surprised to see she needed a little break. When Mona didn't come back to the wall after a couple minutes, I turned around and saw she had tears in her eyes. Obviously, something had come up for her, which came as a surprise. Moments earlier, the room had been riding a wave of incredible energy, and I thought we were in such a good place. I asked Mona if she would share with the team what was going on for her.

Mona said she thought all this effort would be wasted. She didn't believe her leadership would follow through with any of the necessary changes we'd been discussing, and those changes went deep into the identity of the IT organization.

Mona did not trust her leaders to make the required investment to create and sustain change over time.

When she said these words out loud, it was as if all the air had been sucked out of the room and replaced with a truth about the executive leadership that this team of directors was now able to recognize. In this moment, I saw evidence of different values and measures of success at play, and the impact such conflict had on Mona's motivation. She collapsed, unable to go on if she couldn't act in integrity with herself.

The five other people in the group all pulled up chairs making a circle with Mona and sat down quietly. No one disagreed with Mona's assessment. I listened as the team talked about how they wanted to handle the situation, and I was struck by their intrinsic motivations. Mona and her peers were accountable to their direct reports and felt a deep sense of responsibility to them; they were responsible for delivering clarity, inspiration, and truth. They said there was no way they could go back to their teams and pitch this kind of change if they didn't believe the executives would see it through.

From my vantage point, as someone who had worked directly with many of their senior executives and their CIO, Anusha, I was acutely aware of the chasm between these senior directors and the senior executives. Everyone I worked with at this company made indelible marks on my heart and my soul because of how much they cared about the individuals and the company. But the senior executives interacted with a much smaller number of individuals from the team on a day-to-day basis. They were more dependent on metrics and charts and dashboards to understand how the transformation was taking shape. These tools provided an abstract representation of the team's progress, but they did not reflect the work of any individual. Furthermore, the executives were accountable to the board of directors and shareholders. They were making different kinds of decisions and for different reasons.

The senior directors, on the other hand, were interacting with the individuals on their teams daily, and witnessed the cognitive, psychological, and cultural friction in real time. They didn't use that language to describe what their teams were experiencing, but they dealt with the dysfunction of people operating outside their windows of tolerance on a daily basis.

How do we bridge the chasm and blend these two cultures? Making the implicit explicit—calling out the gap, as Mona bravely did—is powerful. It gives people agency to work with the gap or close it. This particular gap was organic, and it made sense. Might it be closed? Perhaps. An alignment existed in the shared awareness of the misalignment. Solutions could be derived if people could see and acknowledge differing values.

I had brought this team to this moment, and it was my responsibility to see it through. That wasn't going to happen in an afternoon; there was deeper work ahead for this client if they wanted to achieve their goals. I needed to reach out to the executive leadership on the other side of the gap and see if we could come to a place of integrity for all.

As it turned out, Anusha, the CIO, shared with me that she was equally frustrated with the senior director team in charge of developing the transformation strategy. Anusha expected the whole IT organization to be further along by now. They'd been working on their transformation long before I entered the picture. There was an undercurrent of mistrust on both sides. To be fair, this kind of transformation is complex. It requires vision, coordination, and dedication. It's very hard for an organization to feel its way through a multiyear transition without a clear pathway, especially without expert guidance.

An alignment existed in the shared awareness of the misalignment

---

To help this client get unstuck, I developed a workshop to promote a shared understanding of what the future could look like and how they might get there. I wanted everyone to have this experience at one time, because the directors and the executives had different roles to play. Since these layers need to work in concert with one another, it's more unifying and powerful if they develop their vision, purpose, identify their values, and develop their processes together.

I didn't magically replace mistrust with trust, but the conditions were created for the directors and the executives to form the culture they needed to achieve their new outcomes. In turn, they created a more productive integration that functioned to maintain as much alignment as possible, to predict where they would run into gaps, and to work around the natural misalignment that came from the different levels at which they worked. Ultimately, the teams adjusted both their values and their outcomes until there was a cogent path between them.

It's wonderful when a team aligns on vision, purpose, and values from the top down at the start of the project. But as you can see, sometimes the need for this alignment ripples up instead. Once the gap has been identified, the clock starts ticking and the work often moves swiftly in profound and effective ways. In this case, and thanks in large part to Mona's contribution and the willingness of both sides to come together, our alignment sessions lasted a total of ten hours. We had an additional eight hours of retros over the next three months to fine-tune the processes that supported business outcomes as well as communication around how values are expressed. They found a way to flow together, in unison, by making the implicit explicit and bridging the gap.

The Contract for Change: Behavioral Norms from the Inside Out

Culture is expressed through behavioral norms, through the choices people make to act or not. To be excruciatingly obvious about this, culture change happens in the hearts, minds, and belief systems of people. Culture changes from the inside out, not the outside in. I'm tempted to fill an entire chapter with only that phrase. It is the single most important concept to understand, so let's unpack what it means.

If people are to accept and embrace change, they need choice. Part of choice is awareness. If you aren't aware there's a new way to do things, or your old habits are so deeply engrained that you forget you have a choice, you lose the opportunity to change your behavior. For people to make choices in accordance with their culture, they need to understand their culture—understand in terms of their belief system, not a recollection of a corporate statement. As we saw with the consultant interviews, telling people what choices to make is ineffective. This is because there are too many unique and unpredictable moments in any one person's day to prepare someone with every possible new response; they need to reason their way to the right answer on their own. Business processes do their best to regulate the big milestones, but how individuals handle interactions, challenges, celebrations, and more is impossible to regulate. But what if you could? Well, you would essentially strip the knowledge from the knowledge worker. There would be no creativity, no ingenuity, no innovation. This is decidedly not what drives growth or change, and it's depressing to even think about!

Organizations and business processes are complex. Even with fixed processes and protocols in place, there are too many unpredictable outside forces. Someone may arrive at a meeting in a foul mood. An angry customer may walk up to the cash register. A new business process may be introduced that impinges on your work. For people to operate in accordance with the culture they desire, they need to be able to act independently and make good judgments.

One key way to intentionally bring vision, purpose, and values into an organization is by defining behavioral norms. This shifts the work from concept to action, creating deliberate moments in which your new culture will come to life.

To ensure people are aware of new choices, I created a contract for change, which is essentially a document that specifies what behavior changes you will make (to literally redefine your culture) and the values those changes reflect. The contract for change also documents what behaviors need to stop because they no longer serve the team or the business.

A contract for change is usually created in a workshop setting so everyone on the team can participate and contribute. There is an example of a contract for change in the back of this book, which illustrates how it can shape behavioral norms that support business outcomes as well as the individuals who are responsible for delivering them. It is an intentional practice to design culture in accordance with business outcomes, and it allows people to find deep connections between their own values, the values of those around them, and the values of the business. This brings people into alignment quickly and helps them be independent right out of the gate. People don't need to learn what a culture—dictated or prescribed—*should* mean to them. They help define it, and nothing is left to interpretation.

If you're embarking on your organization's first ever culture workshop, there will likely be too much information to capture all at once, so I advise creating a first-pass contract to be revisited quarterly to capture new and evolving behavior changes, as well as articulating which behaviors should be eliminated.

I have found the contract for change to be a powerful tool, especially for teams that are geographically distributed and for very large organizations where values vary across teams. In the latter case, I recommend the contract be sent up through the organization so leadership one or two levels up can have a line of sight into what the broader organization needs.

6

Catalysts for Culture Change Are Everywhere

To exist is to change, to change is to mature,
to mature is to go on creating oneself endlessly.
HENRI BERGSON

W E LIVE IN a dynamic world. Sometimes changes are big and the influence on business obvious, and sometimes changes are subtle and the influence on business equally subtle. However, even small influences add up. A multitude of small misalignments can have a big cost on business. You need to keep friction down or it will snowball. To do that, you want to create a sense-and-respond dynamic for your culture because once you experience the benefits of a low-friction environment, you'll want to stay there!

Keeping things in alignment and keeping friction down means adjusting culture. Occasionally this will take some effort. However, once there is substantial alignment, maintaining it can come down to a matter of regularly reviewing purpose and values, mining them for misalignments, and searching for untapped synergy. Once you get the hang of this work, it can be quick and easy to adjust—in some cases, in an hour or less. The potential pain and negative impacts on operations and business outcomes you avoid will be well worth the time you invest.

If you find that no changes are needed, your time was not wasted. You have the assurance that your organizational culture fully supports the team and business outcomes. There are two categories of evidence that suggest the need to review your culture. The first is existing friction in the system. The second is anything that requires a shift in business outcomes and thus values. Before we look at some examples, let's talk about why it's better to keep your finger on the pulse of culture and change as you go. You can sense when it's time for business outcomes to change and get ahead of it, or you can wait until friction arises and then address it. Which would you prefer?

Negative Bias Amplifies Friction

Our three types of friction (cognitive, psychological, and cultural) all include some discomfort or downright pain. With this comes negative sentiment in those carrying the pain. Negative sentiment can spiral downward, and this is especially true when people feel targeted, wounded, or devalued.

I don't want to paint too dark a picture, but we've all heard the phrase "toxic culture." Chances are you have worked in one. They are far too prevalent. And while they can arise from negative forces, they can also be the result of an outdated culture. Working in a toxic culture is something no one should have to tolerate. "Toxic" describes something that will eventually end someone's life! This should drive home the depth of pain and struggle bad culture can cause people, which impacts your bottom line and product quality. And it should underscore how deeply culture is experienced. No amount of additional vacation time, spending allowances, company tchotchkes, or charitable work can change the experience of a person who feels they are being taken for granted, they are under threat, or their core beliefs are unimportant. Thankfully, not all misalignment causes toxic culture, but I've found misalignment in all the toxic cultures I've helped correct.

Something to keep in mind is negativity bias. In a 2008 paper published in *Psychological Bulletin* titled "Not All Emotions Are Created Equal: The Negativity Bias in Social-Emotional Development," negativity bias is described as the idea that negative experiences have a greater impact on people than positive experiences. This is important because people can unwittingly contribute to the amplification of a negative culture. The article discusses evidence that people use positive and negative information in asymmetrical ways; people display "the propensity to attend to, learn from, and use negative information far more than positive information." Negative stimuli is perceived as more complex, and the paper shares the hypothesis that sensing and learning from negative stimuli was protective and therefore evolutionarily advantageous. It does make sense. An antelope hears a rustle in the long grasses of an African savanna. Running leads to survival, whereas pausing to ponder if the rustling is caused by a predator or by something harmless could be detrimental.

It goes back to the signals sent to the amygdala. Our bodies are wired to protect us from harm. Though we live in incredible safety compared to our ancient ancestors, our brains don't care. They look for threat and weight negative data differently than positive data. That's why repair is so important: you don't want the negative data to be the last signal to the amygdala. Because the positive data is weighted differently, we need more of it to outweigh the negative signals. The negative holds our attention, even after it's gone, as a means of protecting us from future threat.

Inside Out: Catalysts from the Team

Two true signals of friction in the system are when individuals and teams aren't delivering outcomes, and everyone is working a level or two lower than their actual jobs. Leaders, if you've made your vision clear and you still need to or are compelled to handhold your team, pay close attention to this section.

Before I started consulting with the software squad, the designers had been escalating problems to Melanie (VP of Design). One of the recurring issues was that they were given very detailed specifications, down to the designs of pages. This scenario placed the designers in the position of "pixel monkeys"; their roles were reduced to moving visual elements around on the page to make sure things line up. There was no expertise required. When the team wasn't being steamrolled, they had the opposite problem: they were given too little information to go on. Either way, they felt set up for failure.

As a team of professionals, they knew what they needed: a seat at the table earlier in the process. Their contributions about customer experience needed to be brought to the attention of their cross-functional teammates, so it could be built into the process. When that didn't happen, the design team's contributions, which should have been generative in nature, became transactional. Try as they might, the team struggled to be heard and involved early in the process, which had yet to be defined.

Furthermore, Carol (VP of Software) put a great deal of pressure on the team to execute quickly because she wanted the board of directors to see that she was turning things around. No one felt like they could pause for a few days to design a better cross-functional process. Every day, Barry (VP of Product), Ethan (CTO), Melanie, or Carol wanted to see what had happened in the previous twenty-four hours. Mei (product owner) often worked at night to communicate her specifications to the design team by the morning, which she usually delivered in drawings or sketches to move things along faster.

The team escalated to Melanie that they needed to get involved with Mei earlier in the process. Melanie did her best to work with Barry and Ethan to create this space for her team, which would allow them to contribute the right work at the right time and to guide Mei on how best to work together. This system worked for a few weeks, but then the team lost traction because the underlying values were misaligned, and there wasn't much of a vision to speak of. There was nothing holding together the new way of working. Every time the team slid backward, the executives moved in a little closer. Eventually, many of the senior executives were down in the weeds. Because of the power differential between the doers and the leaders, the doers took every statement from the leaders as marching orders. However, when the executives started acting more like doers than leaders, no one was leading anymore.

With the software squad, there was a lot of cognitive friction. There was no agreed-upon process or clarity around roles, which created a knowledge gap. When people tried to close it, they negatively impacted their colleagues' abilities to do their jobs, and the friction rippled up to the executive ranks. They, in turn, failed to understand why the team wasn't executing more innovative ideas and came to the incorrect assumption that the team was incapable. The executives stepped in to drive more closely, leaving their leadership posts partially vacant. This also caused psychological friction because people felt they were being treated as incapable, but they did not dare speak up. The cognitive and psychological friction between the design team and the executives was the catalyst for a much-needed cultural change. Thankfully once that catalyst had been named and identified, we facilitated the necessary changes relatively quickly and painlessly.

Outside In: External Catalysts

We've examined quite a few internal catalysts, and now we'll look at a few external factors that can trigger a review of business culture. When outside forces require internal changes, you've probably thought:

- What does this mean for my business?
- What does this mean for how we work?
- What does this mean for how roles are defined and who's in these roles?
- What does this mean for the leadership?

There are dozens of examples of outside-in catalysts for change in business outcomes and how they are achieved. Here are some common ones.

Changes in Your Industry Brought About by the Introduction of New Technology

Current examples of new tech include artificial intelligence at large, ChatGPT, cloud technology and services, and applications that change how people work, like Slack and Trello.

New technology, especially before its uses are fully understood and effectively used, ushers in all kinds of uncertainty for the business and the employees. Businesses are trying to figure out how the technology can improve relationships with customers or the bottom line. Employees are wondering how the technology will impact their professional identities and what it means for day-to-day processes. Some want to be a part of defining technology's impact on the business, and they dive in. For others, their sense of safety is threatened at the prospect of having to learn a new skill, or they fear losing their sense of seniority as their role morphs into something new. Some worry they will be displaced or replaced. This latter group usually digs in their heels to resist adoption of the new technology, which results in behaviors that reveal friction and beget toxic cultures.

Recall when the Apple unveiled the App Store to the world. Old-school brick-and-mortar industries awkwardly ventured into the app race, and this method of connecting with customers represented a host of new business outcomes and values. This was especially true for long-standing businesses such as banks, insurance providers, department stores, and hotel and hospitality chains. Global tech disruptions create an evolutionary loop between overall societal culture and the specific changes necessary for businesses working with the technology.

When big technology companies or startups roll out new products and services, and the value of those contributions become apparent, they ricochet throughout consumer experiences in various ways. As consumers' experiences are enhanced by technology, consumers provide feedback, and the technology is further enhanced. At first, the changes are big as the technology and optimal user base are finding each other and getting acquainted. Eventually, a solid relationship is built between the two, and we see that emerge in culture. From my vantage point, which has been through user observation and research, cultural changes are first seen in consumer expectations of the technology and, on the human side, in how people relate to one another and to brands.

When the iPhone made the App Store available to the general population, people had access to just about anything they wanted, any time, in real time. Overnight, the whole world could transfer money, read about the best restaurants in Bora-Bora, change a flight reservation, identify a song playing in the background of a bar, find a public restroom, or learn what kind of tree they were sitting under at the park—all from their phone. The knowledge of the world was suddenly in our hands, and we could access it whenever we wanted. Of course, this is now a fact of life people have come to demand, and the world has dramatically changed because of it.

From a cultural standpoint, people started to expect that every brand they cared about, specifically the relevant and modern ones, would have a digital presence. And most did. People expected those brands to know them, be responsive to their desires, and predict their desires over time. I've worked with many retailers, banks, hospitality companies, and local governments that fell into the "irrelevant" category, and they struggled under the weight of this change. Like Always Home, their internal business and IT operations were not structured to be responsive. They were structured to disseminate *to*, not converse *with* their customers.

This is why being on top of culture in the face of constant technological innovation is critical. As soon as the next new thing hits the masses, businesses need to be ready to respond. The faster that they can act on information and understand what it means to the company vision, purpose, values, and people, the more relevant they will be. You don't need to be on the bleeding edge of adoption, but you must be ready and able to adapt your culture to new outcomes the moment they start to take shape.

While leading design in the consulting organization, my right arm Rich and I built a self-learning design organization. We helped enterprises adopt technology, which meant we needed to stay a step ahead of its value for the different industries with which we worked. Most of the designers were meeting with clients on the forefront of digital transformation and cloud adoption. We were mining for the identity changes and friction points as they happened and sharing them in our quarterly team calls. By studying and sharing the human behavior patterns we observed, we could see change coming and respond accordingly. By all accounts, design was leading the business. These were incredibly sensitive, talented, intuitive, creative people and I have the utmost respect for them. In a highly dynamic environment, we developed a culture that continued to reinvent our part of the business and inform the rest, as often as necessary.

Eventually, the pace of major technological advances settles down. But in the early days of major change, be prepared to revisit your culture and do the work to realign it to business outcomes every three months. It's energizing and refreshing to implement frequent, small changes periodically. It's unsettling and disruptive to overhaul your culture every few years.

Changes in the Marketplace Brought About by Existing Competitors

If your competition makes big moves faster and more easily than you, you will always be playing catch-up. You want to stay on top of your competition and their impact on the market. Over the course of several years, Airbnb was shifting the hospitality market right under Carol's nose. It wasn't until the pain reached a high enough pitch that Carol acted. We could also say the same thing about the shift to extended stay hotels. Carol was able to respond to that a bit faster because it wasn't so far from Always Home's existing culture and business model.

People want to work for a winning company, partly because winning feels great but also because catching up is hard. When competitors release a game-changing feature or product, especially if no one saw it coming, employees question their leadership's vision. You want to be on the other side of that equation. If you do find yourself in reaction mode, as you shift your business outcomes to get ahead of the competition, remember to investigate your three pillars, because you likely have some updating to do. Examine your culture. Does it drive customer outcomes? How did you slide behind, and what do you need to become a market leader and stay there? I've worked with hundreds of businesses, and they've all found themselves in this position at some point. Culture can help lead you to more nimble, well-informed pastures. Finally, discuss friction points with your teams, especially the leadership team. It is their responsibility to set direction. If the business starts missing big moves in the market, some friction may have crept in; that friction has people taking their gazes away from the business so they can navigate their invisible mazes.

Changes in the Marketplace Brought About by New Competition or Changes in Customers

Remember, Carol (VP of Software) did not originally think Airbnb was a competitor because it was just a technology platform. She didn't take her eye off the ball (her traditional competitors) for a second, but someone threw a new Airbnb ball onto the court! For a time, she thought that little Ping-Pong ball couldn't cause any harm. It's possible to miss innovation if there's a large chasm between the new idea and the business you've been running for twenty years—say, the chasm between a technology platform and fully staffed physical locations.

Carol was caught off guard because her hotel chain was a staple in the hospitality industry, catering to families and businesses alike. However, as the children of her hotel's clients grew up, Carol and Barry (VP of Product) never actually targeted them as customers. Suddenly, those children were spending money, having families of their own, and traveling as young adults. Carol and Barry lost touch with them.

The hotel chain became less relevant to the younger demographic because it didn't understand the profiles, needs, and desires of that clientele well enough. Airbnb recognized this demographic was different. They saw an opportunity in the market, seized it, and permanently changed the hospitality industry. As Jeffrey (senior designer), Jo (lead designer), and Arun (the early career designer) became more embedded with Mei (product owner) earlier in the process, they were able to bring the voice of that demographic into the hearts and minds of the cross-functional team.

When new competition comes on to the scene and is successful—more successful than you—it's time to look at why you missed the opportunity. This situation need not happen often, if ever. Hire a good design team to stay in touch with your users and facilitate relationships between your designers and product owners. Occasionally interview people who are not your typical users, so you can learn about factors you wouldn't normally encounter. It's better to dismiss irrelevant information than miss critical information. Bring that data back into your business through the three pillars and keep one eye fixed on the horizon.

Product or Business Integration Efforts

All large companies identify duplicative efforts occurring across and within departments. These can arise from acquisitions or from management teams that turn a blind eye to bloat. Or maybe management consolidates the portfolio every few years to remain trim and agile. Product and departmental integration often shift business outcomes as product portfolios and features or functions change. In some cases, these changes are merged with changes in business models to create the best conditions for the new portfolio to thrive.

Using the So That method as a means for guiding integration efforts helps pull together the right features and dismiss those that are not core to your value proposition. Product teams all have slightly different cultures, so it's great to follow up with the three pillars to establish the right priorities for the team. If you've gone through all the challenges of proposing product or business unit integrations, which can impact people's professional identities, make sure your three pillars are crisp and understood by everyone before you expect the team to be productive. The people are the ones who will execute on the vision of integration—set them up for success.

It's better to dismiss irrelevant information than miss critical information

Responding to Shifts in Business Models

In almost every industry, information technology organizations in businesses have dealt with shifting delivery methods from on-premises products to a SaaS subscription and delivery model, adopting agile or lean product development methodologies, or shifting to micro services architecture. It can take years for an organization to fully mature with any of these shifts, which means values shift monthly or quarterly for quite some time.

A non-IT example of this shift is the COVID-19 pandemic, which brought about the widespread phenomenon of working from home. Working from home for roughly two years changed people. Those who craved being with people again happily chose to return to the office. Those who appreciated no longer commuting and being able to work in a quiet space, while keeping up with chores and only having to be presentable from the waist up, were not going back to the office if they could help it. In response, leaders had to figure out the right models to help their teams be as effective as possible. This required putting new processes and technologies in place to facilitate creativity, communication, alignment, and delivery. Leaders also needed to make sure this business model appealed to the right talent so they could grow their businesses.

If you are a company that has transitioned from an in-office way of working to a work-from-home or hybrid model, you will benefit from reviewing the three pillars and their culture through the exercises in this book or from running a workshop. In a *Harvard Business Review* article from 2021 titled "WFH Doesn't Have to Dilute Your Corporate Culture," Pamela Hinds and Brian Elliott write, "Many leaders are stymied when it comes to creating and directing culture when employees are far-flung. The first hurdle is acknowledging that culture can no longer be forged in the same way as it was in an office-centric model."

Culture and its signals are different across all three of ways of working. Doing the work in this book will help you make the implicit explicit, so everyone understands the team's values, as well as the behavioral norms they drive. Pay special attention to hybrid ways of working, because that can create a clash of cultures. I agree with Hinds and Elliott, who suggest that a remote-first approach is more inclusive.

Shifts in Overall Culture

Shifts in the wider culture can be caused by a variety of events. To continue with the pandemic example, the resulting Great Resignation saw people leaving their jobs in droves. They realized their organizations were not aligned with their beliefs and values. The sacrifices of working the way they had been and the overall dissatisfaction were too great to endure. Living in fear of, or perhaps recovering from, a deadly virus, losing family and friends, and helping children navigate such dramatic events changed how people perceived their own agency and what they wanted in return for their time, efforts, and talent. The money being exchanged for these things seemed inadequate. The bar for satisfaction, joy, and purpose has been set higher, and tolerance for poor culture lower. Also, social media and gig culture have opened new avenues of opportunity for people, giving them somewhere to go outside the traditional work model. Businesses can respond to these societal shifts by adapting business outcomes and cultural environments to engage, align, and retain talent.

Geographical or Political Influences

For those of us in the United States, we are unaccustomed to experiencing major disruptions (such as the pandemic) on a regular basis. Yet in many other parts of the world, these kinds of disruptions and threats are an everyday part of life and have been for generations.

I once ran a culture workshop within an organization to align values and repair trust so the team could improve its operational efficiency. Team members were in the Americas, Europe, and Asia. When we signed in for the workshop, we learned that several of the team members in Asia were impacted by a political conflict that had flared up with a neighboring country. These team members and their families were under direct threat; they even traveled armed for protection. The region's infrastructure had also been impacted, and they were confined to working via their smartphones, unable to use the collaboration tools we planned to leverage. The worldviews of these team members were quite different from the worldviews of the team members on the West Coast of the United States, for example, who had just rolled out of bed for the 7:30 a.m. virtual workshop, still in their pajamas and sipping their morning coffee.

I was aware of the political strife in that part of Asia, but I did not realize the direct impact it had on the team members. When the reality of what they were coping with came to light, we paused the planned agenda to check in with them. We offered to change the workshop dates, which they declined. This team was ready to do what was needed to improve the organization's overall culture. We made time for them to share their real-world experiences and challenges, both so we could both empathize with what they were going through and to adjust the workshop. We wanted them to be able to participate and collaborate at the same level as the rest of the team, even while constrained to using their smartphones.

The Asian team members were not only experiencing cognitive and psychological friction from the political strife, but they were also under direct threat (having to carry firearms for safety). Had we not openly brought this situation into the workshop for everyone to see and understand, we would have exacerbated the cultural friction that already existed among three different geographies with different cultures. As the rest of the team got their minds around the experiences of their Asian colleagues, hearts opened and people became generous with their time and their efforts, going out of their way to make things as easy as possible. And remember, this was a team that was not in a great place to begin with. The purpose of the workshop was to repair trust.

As the workshop progressed, hearts remained open. People heard and understood one another more deeply and committed to increasing their efforts to create a trusting place where everyone's contributions were valued.

First Bank of Old Family Money: Internal and External Catalysts

Let's look at a real-world example of internal and external catalysts that necessitated values and culture change within an organization. If you have ever been through a reorganization with a business that is reinventing itself or modernizing, some of this may be familiar. All names have been changed, including the players and the organization.

As its name suggests, First Bank of Old Family Money had been catering to the same clientele for over one hundred years.

For decades, parents put their wealth into the hands of their children through Old Family Money's fiduciary and trust services. When baby boomers began to pass away, Old Family Money saw its business was shrinking.

In an overall culture shift (external catalyst), a portion of the Gen X and millennial generations had moved on to more modern banking experiences, which were primarily digital and highly personalized. These generations were mostly banking from their phones; stepping into a bank was a major inconvenience. This was the opposite of previous generations, whose banking experiences were informed by their relationships with the tellers and brokers who worked in the physical bank located in their neighborhood. Family wealth was being transferred out of Old Family Money and into the new digital-first banks or banks with more sophisticated digital services.

Old Family Money took action to lean into the culture shift. They learned what made Gen Xers and millennials tick, what brands they valued and why, and what they were looking for in money management. Over a few years, Old Family Money's efforts paid off, and the numbers were coming back. Yet the bank seemed to have two separate arms: one for the retiring generation and one for the younger generations, the digital-first seekers. The business was only going to grow in one direction, so the bank decided it was time to restructure internally to prepare for its future.

This is one of the hardest changes to make because both sides of the business were still serving customers: the bank couldn't shutter one side of the house in favor of the other. As product teams integrated with each other, they needed to figure out how to make decisions. Everyone knew that the future was digital and the traditional business would eventually fold into the digital side. This impacted employees' professional identities and they felt bereft and unvalued (internal catalyst of existing friction). Notice that we have both internal and external catalysts for change. If Old Family Money had caught the external catalysts early enough and built a strong vision, they would have reduced the internal catalyst and the amount of psychological and cognitive friction it caused.

Let's compare the values of the two arms of the bank. The bank had always tried to value what its customers valued, which is why it had been in business for over a century. Because of this, we will look at the values of the two different types of clients.

Because its customers have two sets of values, the bank experiences two different sets of internal values for the two product teams.

With client values pointing in opposite directions, we can see that the product teams make decisions from different places and toward different ends. Most reorganizations are for the long-term health of the business and have the potential to create chaos up front because of misaligned values. At Old Family Money, not only are values misaligned between the teams, they are also misaligned from the standpoint of the bank's identity. The misalignment is necessary because the bank is preparing for *what it will become*, as they should so they don't end up in the position of Always Home.

Old Family Money needs to look at what the company will become, define those values, and chart a pathway for everyone to get there in a way that is minimally disruptive to its existing clients and employees. We know that one demographic will get smaller over time and the other will grow. The bank is right to reorganize because it allows the whole team to intentionally drive the bank's future to realize its future incarnation.

Retiring Client Values	Digital-First Client Values
Prefers personal relationships and builds trust in the bank's brand by talking to human beings.	Prefers to act autonomously and only interact with a human on their terms for specific requests.
Predictability. If change must happen, it should be minor or undetectable.	Accepts change readily if there is value. Will take to social media to voice displeasure.
Artifacts in hand. Mistrust of digital assets.	Wants data at their fingertips: checking balances at the beach, depositing checks from the couch.
Wants their bank to have specific knowledge of them: birthday, where money is spent, marital status. Mistrusts the leveraging of data to sell products or categorize spending. Using that data crosses a boundary.	Wants their bank to know and understand its users, make suggestions, and always improve user experience and value.
Has more of a separation between business and personal values.	Wants the values of service and product providers to be aligned with their personal values.

Retiring Client Product Team Values	Digital-First Client Product Team Values
Steady as she goes! Changes happen only when something breaks or there is value to add. Changes happen on predictable schedules and are announced first through in-branch advertising.	Digital assets are updated with new value and personalization multiple times a week or even multiple times a day.
Annual survey. Customers don't want changes and don't want to be bothered.	Leverage big data to stay on top of customer behavioral trends to provide continued value and personalization.

By establishing the vision of its future and defining the purpose and values to drive that future identity, the bank can work backward and establish reasonable milestones for team and product integration. That's important if you want to get somewhere specific and track your progress along the way. It's extremely valuable for employees because they can see the throughline of their relevance and when it would be good to reskill or move to another team within the bank. At each milestone, employees can prepare for the next milestone by adjusting their values and outcomes to ensure they reach it. Because this is a long-term shift, the activities used to do this work can be repeated as often as needed (but certainly every milestone or two) to stay in alignment with each other and the needs of the business.

First Bank of Old Family Money was able to successfully navigate both the internal and external catalysts for change by going about its cultural design both preemptively and intentionally. They saw the dangers heading their way and got ahead of them. Though it took some work to get the two product teams on the same page, once everyone was aligned to the future longevity of the bank, they worked to keep the bank relevant.

Changes in business outcomes or how they are achieved can come from anywhere at any time, from inside or outside the company. Awareness of potential internal and external catalysts of friction is the best defense for heading that disruption off at the pass.

7

Leadership: The Most Important Ingredient for Culture

In matters of style, swim with the current; in matters of principle, stand like a rock.
THOMAS JEFFERSON

WHEN IT comes to leadership, there is no neutral, no zero on the number line. Leaders both set the tone and have the final say about the culture of their organizations. In "The Impact of Leadership Styles on Organizational Culture and Team Effectiveness," published in the *Journal of Management and Organization*, authors Andrew S. Klein, Joseph Wallis, and Robert A. Cooke tell us that part of the leader's role is to leverage their "authority to challenge existing norms that may impede the achievement of corporate goals." Leaders ensure alignment with outcomes. They help team members create resiliency during challenging times. They demonstrate behavioral norms and give permission when those norms need to change.

When leaders create the conditions in which their teams thrive, their teams bring the wisdom they've gained throughout their careers to bear on achieving the organization's business outcomes, and they extend that wisdom across the organization. This helps people feel highly valued with a deep attachment between their purpose and the organization's purpose, and purpose is the ultimate motivation.

Or... leadership can leave gaping holes in business processes, improperly staff or inform employees and teams, and allow conflicting business models to wreak havoc on the success and welfare of the company. Through their daily behavior, leaders choose what values and beliefs are rewarded and indicate how team members should respond to values, beliefs, and behaviors that are not welcome.

When leaders do not act in accordance with the stated organizational values, they communicate that they don't believe in the values, or they don't believe the values apply to them. Even if that is not the intended message, it calls the leader's integrity and trustworthiness into question. (Heather gave me a heads-up before I went too far down this path.) By doing this, leaders communicate it's okay to disregard commitments made to the team and to the business (as we saw in Mona's experience). When leaders demonstrate values other than the ones the team has agreed upon, or they do not make the new values explicit, teams yo-yo between trying to transform and resorting back to old behaviors and cultural expectations.

Individual decisions by leaders establish culture. Leaders, you don't want to establish culture in a vacuum, or you'll miss opportunities to tap into intrinsic motivation, which is why I collected the exercises found at the back of this book. You and your teams ought to define the culture together. Since culture expresses the values needed to accomplish the business's outcomes, everyone should be in lockstep. You may have some differing values across organizational layers or across teams, but, as we discussed, this is because these layers or teams contribute differently to the outcome. In Chapter 6, we talked about the catalysts that introduce culture change. Leaders, in this regard, you want to be a step ahead so you can clear the way for change.

Servant Leadership

The strategies and exercises in this book work nicely with the concept of servant leadership. The core of servant leadership puts a premium on service to the community. The team does a different job than the leader; they know best what is needed to accomplish the outcome you as the leader expect. With a little help from the stories and strategies you've read about so far, you can easily work together to design the culture the team needs.

The term "servant leadership" was coined by Robert K. Greenleaf, a lineman for AT&T who worked his way into management. He spent decades researching management and development, and upon retirement, he founded the Greenleaf Center for Servant Leadership. In his famous essay on the topic, "The Servant as Leader," Greenleaf writes,

> The servant-leader is servant first... It begins with the natural feeling that one wants to serve, to serve first. Then conscious choice brings one to aspire to lead. That person is sharply different from one who is leader first, perhaps

> because of the need to assuage an unusual power drive or to acquire material possessions... The leader-first and the servant-first are two extreme types. Between them there are shadings and blends that are part of the infinite variety of human nature.

It takes courage to be the person or group of people who champions change. We can feel at risk or exposed, which generates its own cognitive and psychological friction. I mention this to be extremely transparent. Take stock of your comfort level with servant leadership, especially if you find yourself frustrated with the idea of having to serve, or you want to be the one with all the answers.

The team needs to define the culture that will help them thrive; you, as the leader, give them permission to do so by providing the space, time, methods, and vision. Organizational leaders and their team members have *different roles and jobs* and need different things to create the conditions for success (like Mona and her peers, as compared to Anusha and her peers). For sure, there should be shared values. But one cannot define the values and beliefs needed to achieve the outcomes of others. You must be crystal clear about the business outcomes you expect and overcommunicate them on a regular basis in a way that fosters dialogue. By doing this, you and the team ensure you understand each other, there is no ambiguity, and you give your team the best opportunity to deliver on those outcomes.

If servant leadership is not your strength and you are not interested in it or able to embrace it, surround yourself with people who do. The exercises at the back of the book are about the effective care and feeding of your team's psychology and culture. This means *attending to* the team, not *telling* the team. Consider this further explanation from the Greenleaf Center website:

> A servant-leader focuses primarily on the growth and well-being of people and the communities to which they belong. While traditional leadership generally involves the accumulation and exercise of power by one at the "top of the pyramid," servant leadership is different. The servant-leader shares power, puts the needs of others first, and helps people develop and perform as highly as possible.

A new leader by the name of Soo embodied servant leadership in her behavior, her attitude, and in her heart. This is her story, and I got to witness it.

Soo's Leadership Test

In the early 2000s, there was not much data about design's valuable impact or its importance to user interface. It was all so new. I was on a design team where, unfortunately, everyone felt downtrodden, disempowered, and devalued, a common experience of many design teams at that time. We routinely had to argue, cajole, and convince larger technical teams of our value, and we felt demoralized to see our hard work dismissed every day by our colleagues. Soo was familiar with our situation because she was on an adjacent team, which was treated in much the same ways as ours.

One day, Soo heard there was going to be an opening for a new manager on our team. She hoped that whoever was hired would be a great leader who understood design. We needed someone who could shift our design team's hearts and minds into a place of empowerment. Once we were properly supported and encouraged, we could set an example for other teams.

But Soo did not expect what happened next. The departing manager reached out and asked her to apply for the role. Soo had zero confidence she could deliver on her own aspirations, but she loved our team, and she knew what a huge impact we could have on the business by helping everyone more deeply understand their users and their problems. Soo decided to apply for the job and was selected.

Once in the role, she set about trying to shift our culture. She wanted to empower us to believe in our own agency and value. Soo started this shift by setting up one-on-one meetings with every team member. She met with Bobby first. He had been with the company for more than a decade and was known for his top-notch research and design skills and for building valuable relationships with his customers. Soo had worked with him early in her career when she first joined the company. During their meeting, Bobby told her, "I just want to put in my eight hours and go home." It turned out that Bobby had received the lowest rating possible in his year-end review and was on a performance improvement plan. Soo was surprised.

Why was Bobby, who was widely regarded as a capable high performer, on a performance plan? It didn't make any sense. He was the one who had helped Soo learn the ropes and establish herself. He was the person young designers turned to when they were stuck. He always had a fresh approach or a creative idea. Soo knew his design work was deeply aligned with his sense of purpose. But as Bobby's role and contributions had been devalued, along with most of the rest of the design team, he felt personally devalued, which created psychological friction that weighed on him every day. After a while, he was worn down and depleted. He disengaged from his job and turned inward. If Bobby did not reach his improvement plan's goals, he could easily lose his job. This company was famous for annual layoffs to reduce headcount.

Soo was not about to let Bobby be diminished or put his career with the company in jeopardy. She was determined to illuminate a pathway to greater success for him if he was willing to reinvigorate his role. Because she was the one asking, Bobby agreed to give it a try.

The first thing Soo did was put Bobby on a highly visible, high-priority product with another designer. His sense of purpose was aligned with the importance of the project, and the visibility of the project boosted Bobby's sense of value. Bobby also had the support of his colleagues; in his previous project, he had been the only designer (never a good practice, as design is highly collaborative). Soo and Bobby got together weekly, and Soo made sure to provide Bobby with air cover during controversial moments so he could get his ideas and research on the table. Bobby felt supported again, and after a short time, he completely turned his situation around. He was leading a small team, and both customers and technical teams alike recognized and praised his work. Bobby told Soo, "You make me want to come to work and do a good job. That wasn't the case a few months ago, so thank you." His words were a defining moment of Soo's career. She felt deeply rewarded for helping to create an environment in which Bobby could thrive again.

Fast-forward a few months. The company was preparing for its annual layoffs. Each manager had to nominate 9 percent of their team for dismissal. The message cascaded down from Soo's manager with the spreadsheet where the names of layoff candidates were to be entered. In someone's mind, this strategy seemed equitable. To Soo, it was anything but. She couldn't help but wonder if this arbitrary approach to cost savings would ultimately help or harm the business. She was convinced a reprioritization of projects could help the company achieve its commitments to its customers and to Wall Street. And her experience with Bobby showed her they were in danger of losing top talent if the organization continued to be mismanaged.

Soo questioned the layoff approach with her peers and her manager, saying it was wildly unfair to the employees. Some of her peers urged her to get on board with the company's method, saying things like "This is the way we've always done it" and "You're not going to change the company." Some people implied Soo's first alliance should be to her peers rather than to the people on her team. They believed if they were forced to sacrifice some of their direct reports, then she should too. These conversations looped around over the course of a few weeks.

Soo's team—the only design team designated for this suite of products—was made up of only eight people in an organization of hundreds. Each one of them was making demonstrable impacts under challenging circumstances. Soo argued this point, along with the negative impact her team would suffer if she was forced to cut a member.

One of Soo's peers suggested she put Bobby's name on the spreadsheet. It was customary, after all, to let poor performers go. Whoever had put him on a performance plan didn't know how hard Bobby and Soo had worked to get his engine restarted, and restart it he did. Bobby was getting great feedback from customers. There was no way she could put his name on the list—or anyone else's, for that matter.

The call for layoffs forced Soo to examine her core values and what she believed the purpose of her role as a manager was. Was she there simply to execute her manager's orders, or was she there to develop a high-performing team that achieved great business outcomes? And what did her peers think their roles were as managers? It seemed values were misaligned, just when alignment was needed the most. When this misalignment snapped into focus for Soo, she felt a cold rush of fear. And she felt alone. According to her peers' comments, success in this role meant she was there for management, and that's not what she had signed up for.

When Soo's boss pushed her for a name to contribute to the layoff, she numbly responded, "I have no one to add." After a pause, her manager said, "If you don't pick someone, I will." As kindly as she could muster, Soo replied, "If that's what needs to happen, I understand. But I need to do what I believe is right. No one on this team is a poor performer, so I don't have a name to give you."

A couple weeks later, the final spreadsheet of layoff candidates was released, and no one from Soo's team was on the list. She was gobsmacked. She hadn't considered this as an option. She expected to see Bobby's name on the spreadsheet along with formal HR documentation about her disobedient conduct. Her manager was the final decision-maker on this matter, and she had his support. This meant a lot to her.

Through the experience, Soo learned she could trust herself, even when caught up in a system that did not fit her values. If Bobby's job had been eliminated, Soo had acted in accordance with her values, which made her values visible to those around her. And she was not alone. Obviously, her manager either agreed with her or respected her decision as a manager. He did not interfere with her decision, and a larger change started to take root.

A few years later, when Soo was put up for promotion, her manager wrote a strong letter of recommendation. He specifically highlighted her ability to change culture by shifting the belief systems of leadership.

While Soo's story is ultimately triumphant, it was an emotionally challenging time for her. She experienced psychological friction caused by the fear that she would have to compromise her integrity and sacrifice a direct report to keep her job. She also experienced cultural friction when she was pressured by her peers and manager to put a name on the spreadsheet. She felt isolated and confused. For many, especially in middle management and below, friction comes down to this choice. Soo was lucky her manager supported her, but the friction she experienced could have been avoided.

Imagine if Soo's manager said, "Team, we must reduce headcount by 9 percent. Let's first prioritize the projects to focus on. With those in mind, let's discuss, as a team, how to do this as fairly as possible." Or he could have asked his team for their recommendations on how best to get to the right-sized organization. This would have had all the managers working to solve the same problem: how to achieve the business's outcomes with 9 percent fewer people. From there, the next step would be to decide how to choose the 9 percent to cut. Laying off people in the context of shifting business priorities is a different conversation than arbitrarily forcing 9 percent out because "it's policy."

Leaders, when you do the work of designing a culture for outcomes, you and your teams will likely be inserting your

The best leaders are not always the people at the top of the org chart

new culture into a bigger system. As you do so, thoughtfully examine what beliefs and values give rise to the larger culture. Like Soo, question institutionalized values. Protect the culture you need for your team to succeed, and give them permission to do the same. When something doesn't feel right, do not assume you are powerless. You may not be able to change the whole system, but you may be able to make a situation right for one person and, in so doing, lead by example and be a light to others.

Acting in ways that demonstrate the new values and norms for your team and those around you gives everyone permission to let go of the old. Soo embraced the principles of servant leadership by working with Bobby to reignite his passion, while creating an environment for him and others to do their best work. She maintained the same principles when it came time to protect her people from layoffs. Let's recognize that by standing firm in her principles, Soo gave her own manager permission to do the same. And later she was rewarded with a promotion for being a catalyst for change. The best leaders are not always the people at the top of the org chart.

The Leadership To-Do List

Leaders' roles are different than the doers' roles, so I'm adding a few special action items for leaders. These actions help you to support your teams by informing you about their needs.

1. Seek to Understand

Deeply understand the team's values and what they envision for the future. The exercises at the back of the book give you access to everything the team is doing, thinking, and feeling.

The "why"—the purpose for the team's answers—is of particular importance, as it will help you learn what motivates the individuals on your team. As a leader, you can help your team go further by tapping into that motivation. As we've seen throughout this book, motivation is not the same from person to person, especially in cross-functional teams. You likely have very talented people in your midst, and servant leaders find ways to unleash that talent and wisdom and motivate their teams to build their own futures.

Your team's responses to the exercises in this book or in a workshop provides you with an excellent opportunity to practice active listening. It can be quite humbling for leaders to see their team create complete landscapes of how they want to achieve the business's outcomes, and it inspires faith and trust between you and your team. While listening to the team's discoveries, you can ensure the organizational mission and business outcomes are what you expected and realign as needed. Then commit to doing your part to change the culture by asking what they need from you. In particular, ask about the communications plan. Depending on the team's vision of its future and how the team operates, you may have some work to do in this area, either with them or with adjacent teams on their behalf. Once you know what should be done and what should no longer be done, make sure to get a contract in place. Revisit the contract regularly to keep it updated.

2. Check In on Purpose and Values

Once your team has walked you through their organizational mission, purpose, and values, make time for some deep reflection on what you heard. As you reflect on the outcomes of the exercises, search for even the smallest levels of friction. Big friction points will be obvious. More subtle friction cues may be detected in your body or emotions before they are processed by your brain's executive functions, if they are processed there at all. Look for small waves of negative feelings such as frustration, irritation, or anger. Friction can also feel like isolation, loneliness, or feeling misunderstood. It bears mentioning that I've seen plenty of leaders exhibit avoidant or even sabotaging behaviors when it comes to doing this work. If you find yourself never quite getting around it, you may be experiencing some anxiety or threat about what you might learn from your team or about yourself. These responses are okay: this is simply data that is valuable for you and your awareness as a leader.

Once you are aware of friction in your organization or within yourself, look for the sources of misalignment. Where there is misalignment, there are likely different values. As we know, there is some misalignment that cannot be removed. But awareness of differently aligned values gives people the ability to plan for it and work around it.

Imagine your team values innovation, and you value speed. Are innovation and speed always opposed to each other? I've heard different responses to this question. Some business leaders think innovation and speed are at odds. They fear the creative task of innovating takes too long, or they feel sufficient innovation has been achieved and they're eager to get to market. Other leaders who are well versed in lean methods and design thinking value rapid ideation, innovation, and user validation. Both can be valued without causing friction, but we need awareness of the differences to find the solution.

What about differences in values or purpose that point in different directions? For example, the waitstaff of a restaurant chain identify customer relationships as a high-priority value. Relationships bring their customers back week after week.

However, the chain's management values maximizing revenue by encouraging customer turnover, and they have metrics for the amount of time a customer should be seated before it's time for the next customer. We can see the friction that management's metrics might introduce for the waitstaff when they are in conflict with their own sense of purpose. In this case, a middle ground can and should be struck that supports the company's high-priority values while delivering positive bottom-line results.

As you find areas of potential derailment, you may not need to make an immediate decision. Use the doable versus valuable exercise in the back of the book. Run experiments and gather more data to determine how to get the outcome you want. Look for areas of constructive collaboration. What excites you? Does it align with what excites your team? Great! Make it a point to find and leverage those areas of commonality to motivate your team and set even more ambitious goals.

3. Update Your Operations

Help your team to execute the contract for change by building the following activities or practices into your operations:

- Budget training or tooling the team needs to reduce cognitive friction.
- Monitor team checkpoints to stay up to speed with their progress.
- Create metrics to measure and reward progress.
- Identify metrics to *stop* measuring to prevent friction or misalignment.

- Constantly scan the horizon for changes to business outcomes or other occurrences that could introduce friction or misalignment.
- Help the team manage friction when their values differ from those of other teams they work with. The exercises in this book help with this.
- Evaluate team member skills and provide education or support where needed.
- Ensure psychological safety—the team should feel comfortable bringing conflicting values to your attention. If needed, chart a journey of repair to get to that point.
- Run regular retrospectives to assess alignment and make sure you and your team are still in lockstep. Iron out any misalignments that may have formed.

Common Pitfalls

Leadership's impact on culture cannot be understated. Friction and misalignment can escalate quickly, but with the right tools and awareness, negative factors can be mitigated and de-escalated just as quickly. In my many years of consulting with individuals at all levels, I've noticed some common pitfalls at the leadership level, especially at the senior executive level. To help you avoid making the same mistakes as others (and indeed some of the same mistakes I've made myself), I've put together a brief list of repeat offenders.

1. Lack of Follow-Through

Lack of follow-through at the leadership level eventually translates into lack of follow-through at *all* levels. When a leader stops supporting an initiative, it sends the signal that the initiative is no longer important. Remember Mona from Chapter 5? She's the one who teared up in frustration, believing that her leadership team would not follow through on the new initiatives she and her peers were working hard to roll out. Her feelings were based on behaviors she'd repeatedly witnessed, and unfortunately, it's a common occurrence. I've seen leaders who are so focused upward, toward their desired outcomes, they overlook or are unaware of how much effort, time, and expense went into achieving them. Even worse is when initiatives or outcomes are introduced with great fanfare and then unceremoniously abandoned without effectively communicating as much to the teams. And then leaders are surprised by the collateral damage to the talent or the toxicity permeated throughout the culture by such behavior.

Ironically, the absence of leadership support introduces a barrier. Even if leadership supported an initiative at the beginning, they stop asking about it once things are running well, which leaves teams feeling taken for granted. This is why retrospectives are so important: they embed culture into operations and help keep all necessary alignments up-to-date.

2. Solving the Wrong Problem

There's an old management saying: "All problems are people problems." By now, you understand the invisible friction that happens inside people and teams and how that impacts your business, as well as what evidence to look for. You're empowered to help your team identify and remove that friction. You may be tempted to blame non-human-driven factors such as the pace of change, the speed of technological development, or outdated systems and processes. Don't allow yourself to get distracted by forces beyond your control. Yes, these factors cause issues for people, so when problems or poor performance occur, the first place to look is your *human system*. Ask people what has changed for them and when. Run through the exercises at the back of the book with an eye on the areas in need of change to help your teams course correct.

3. Staying Put

One thing that may not show up during this work is when leaders feel teams are encroaching on *their* roles. (Did Arty, from the introduction, make you feel this way?) Leaders, you may need to level up.

As teams design their future and how they want to get there, leaders may need to let go of their visions of how the teams would work. This may leave them feeling displaced or adrift. When this happens, leaders may feel unclear about their identity and value. This is a form of psychological friction introduced by the team's growth.

This is excellent news—the business is advancing! Time to grow. Of course, growth feels better when it's your own choice, so frame this as your choice. You gathered the data and now you can choose to advance your purpose to support the business and the team. Reexamine your organizational mission, purpose, and values to see how you can up-level your contribution to them.

4. Ignoring Individuals' Primal Emotions

We have discussed the brain's natural response to threat, the three types of invisible friction, and the many and varied emotional responses people have to uncertainty or ambiguity in their environments. After someone's sense of safety has been threatened and their fear response has been triggered, culture can go awry, and outcomes are less likely to be achieved.

Leaders, you must acknowledge the humanness of the people who work for you and do everything possible to eradicate fear and eliminate confusion. Your goals are to provide:

- Absolute clarity around business outcomes and why those outcomes matter. If outcomes change, explain why.

- Space and time for people to align their personal purpose to the business's outcomes. People feel safer and more engaged when they see themselves in the vision.

- A psychologically safe environment.

Build a game plan to accommodate emotional responses and share it with the whole organization, so everyone can use it as needed. When it comes to disseminating information, maintain consistency across leadership. The more consistent the leadership, the less often differences will arise between teams because there is less potential for the escalation of gossip and negativity.

Leaders, you have special roles. You are under more scrutiny than others. Your choices demonstrate the values of the organization. Contradictions between your behavior and the organization's values engender mistrust, rolling out all three types of friction. When you act in accordance with the values and vision, you are a leader to be followed. Furthermore, you reduce the potential for friction in the system, improving both your outcomes and decreasing the financial and human cost of achieving them.

The techniques in this book are intended to bring transparency to the table. They help teams and organizations engage in defining their own pathways through change in a coordinated fashion, with a sense of agency, and to achieve better results. People usually know their jobs better than their leaders and have a good sense of how to get the desired business outcomes (or very close).

The more transparency you bring to the organization's vision, purpose, and values, the less friction you allow in. Communicate clearly and often about expectations. Create a culture of listening and understanding among your leadership community to facilitate an environment where everyone works in unison.

8

Know Before You Grow: How to Seed a Deep-Rooted Culture

My freedom will be so much the greater and more meaningful the more narrowly I limit my field of action and the more I surround myself with obstacles. Whatever diminishes constraint diminishes strength. The more constraints one imposes, the more one frees one's self of the chains that shackle the spirit.

IGOR STRAVINSKY

IN HIS *Poetics of Music,* Stravinsky penned the words at the top of this chapter in the context of starting from nothing. Where to begin? The experience of the blank page can be daunting. There is nothing to work with and everything to choose from. Stravinsky found freedom and creativity within constraints; the boundaries set him free. This is an important concept to keep in mind as you move through the work of designing a culture for outcomes. There is no perfect organization or culture. There is no moment when everything stops, and you get to hit the refresh button. You will always be working with some form of constraints, and it's good to know how to embrace them. You may not get everything right the first go-around, and that's okay. Even if you did, things would change again. Relax into the process, and know there will always be more opportunity for improvement.

By engaging with the principles of this book and their companion activities (in the back of the book) with transparency and sincerity, culture can make deep roots across an organization in a matter of weeks. This book opened with a story I have seen play out time and again—after just a few weeks, a new culture began to take root within the software squad's design team. Jeffrey (the senior designer), Arun (the early career designer), and Jo (the lead designer) intentionally set about making necessary changes and very quickly. Carlos (the engineering architect), Jiang (the lead developer), and Mei (the product owner) noticed that partnering was easier. The design team developed a culture that removed as much friction as possible.

In our retrospectives, we brainstormed how to handle—with our newly agreed-upon values and culture—conflict that entered the system at the intersection of the design team and the cross-functional teams led by Carlos and Mei. As we did this, the relationships between Mei, Carlos, and the design team improved. The new culture started to spread outward because it was more suited to the outcomes the team was trying to achieve.

After three to four months, the team mastered the evolution of their culture. Part of this included adopting behavioral norms from other teams, which helped them create better conditions for their creativity, co-creation, and communication.

Bridging these cultural boundaries helped the team identify new synergies with some of their cross-functional partners. Over time, the software squad created a culture of iteration, making improvements every few weeks.

The key to this kind of success is remembering that culture is built on values that are embodied by people. It starts inside a person who has a clear understanding of the vision and business outcomes. When people are given agency and the tools to develop a culture *to drive outcomes*, they can embody the values needed to achieve those outcomes. As those values are acted upon, culture fills the organization. This is what happens when culture is intentionally designed, and it's thrilling to witness and experience. Hands down, it is the most meaningful work I've ever had the privilege of doing.

For culture design to go smoothly, I'd like to share some elements you are likely to encounter along the way—some constraints to embrace. Think of it as a "know before you go" guide to get the greatest return on your investment by putting in place the right psychological conditions and staying focused on the right things at the right time. The goal is to build a culture that thrives, and you'll see for yourself how quickly change can happen.

There Will Be Misalignment

One of the most prevalent and important constraints to embrace is that there *will* be misalignment. At every intersection, whether it be between disciplines, teams, organizations, or entire business units, you have differing roles, goals, contributions, and success measurements. You may not be able to align on everything, so your goal is to align on the *right* things.

Culture is built on values that are embodied by people

Right things are those that provide each contributing entity (team, organization) with the best chance of meeting their goals and getting business outcomes, while at the same time minimizing friction.

Misalignment immediately introduces cognitive and psychological friction. The cognitive friction is caused by people not knowing how to make decisions when faced with conflicting priorities. The psychological friction is the result of people not being able to accomplish their goals, by being at odds with coworkers about how to move forward, and even by knowing their work interrupts the work of their colleagues. (We'll see an example of that in a few pages.)

Several of the activities in the back of the book (empathy map, active listening, and business impact worksheet) are specifically designed to draw out areas of misalignment. Where misalignment arises, you call it out and discuss it. In some cases, you can overcome the misalignment. Mona and her colleagues were able to smooth over the misalignment with their executive leadership team by creating a stronger overlap between those two organizational levels wherein information could be exchanged. This created more awareness between the two groups and built enough alignment in key areas to overcome friction.

What about when you cannot remove the misalignment, or you do not have the elegant bridging opportunity Mona and her colleagues had? There are a few things you will want to do: understand each other, mine for conflict, and innovate solutions.

Embrace the Constraints

In this section, we'll look at how understanding, mining for misalignment, and innovation helped a team through one of the most common struggles in a maturing software organization: the creation of a design system. Getting a design system off the ground inherently comes with misalignment. This activity impacts business processes, how people spend their time, and how they manage their budgets. When done right, they are well worth the investment because of the cost savings they provide through operational efficiencies, as well as the benefits to both the customer and the company, which come with consistent user experiences.

The Nielsen Norman Group defines a design system as "a complete set of standards intended to manage design at scale using reusable components and patterns." Design systems are usually shared across an entire company. This ensures that as people design pages, they reuse as much of each other's work as possible.

Mature design organizations have a centrally governed team that implements a matrixed structure to leverage the design and development talent of their colleagues, who submit their work into the design system. These governing teams ensure communication across all areas of design and development so everyone knows what is being created, how to give feedback, and when a submitted element is be ready to use.

Without design systems, we get Frankenstein user interfaces. Pages, the interactions they comprise, and the objects on the page can differ as much as the people who designed and coded them. Without design systems, customers may find inconsistencies and differences with fonts and colors and experience all kinds of unexpected behaviors in pages, buffers, and gutters (the spaces between objects on the page), and how widgets interact. These inconsistencies and differences add cognitive load into the equation. It's hard for people to discern where they are, to recognize actions, to learn, and to comprehend.

Of equal importance, sloppy-looking and sloppy-acting user interfaces impart a negative brand image and experience. In the words of one of my former banking customers, "If I can't trust you with the little stuff like lining things up on a page, how can I trust you with the big stuff, like securing my data?" That remark was made in 2005, and to this day, I still recite it to anyone who will listen. Imagine if your bank's online checking account pages and savings account pages used different colors, fonts, placed their buttons in different places, and labeled a button Continue on one page and OK on another. You would be right to wonder if the people at the bank were talking to one another and what the implications of the answer are for you, their customer.

You might ask, "If design systems are good for the user, good for the brand, and reduce work for designers and developers, where is the misalignment?" In the first months to years, design systems are volunteer efforts. This means people are splitting their time between designing for their product (usually the origin of the component or pattern) and taking feedback and redesigning components until they work for other designers. The same goes for the developers who code the components so they function. Here begins our misalignment.

If you ask each of these teams what their primary outcomes are, their answers would be those generated by the products they put into the world for customers to use. Yet others depend on the components created by these volunteers. The need for consistency and the fact that everyone is using each other's components means there's a vast web of interdependencies throughout product teams.

Moira and her team are responsible for designing and developing a new dashboard for premier credit card users that allows them to set monthly spending limits in a variety of different categories, such as dining out, utilities, vacation, and so on. This feature then alerts the users as they approach those limits.

Bart and his team are responsible for creating a new dashboard where people can specify a savings plan goal, such as a vacation to Aruba for a family of four, and the dashboard visualizes the progress. Bart learns about the spending-limit component Moira is designing. It is very similar to what Bart is doing—one person's limit is another person's goal, after all. Bart goes to the component library, plays around with it, and decides it will work for his savings dashboard.

Several months later, Bart is running some user testing for his application and finds that he needs some changes made to the component, so he reaches out to Moira and her team, who have moved on to other work. They are unable to take this on—the component works fine for them—bringing Bart to a dilemma. His development team could learn how the component works, duplicate the code, and make a second version with the changes they need, so as not to disrupt Moira's application. However, this approach would eat away at the gains his team has made by leveraging an existing component, and it would blow out their schedule.

This kind of situation happens all the time when people share work. Moira and her team are prioritizing their product work, while Bart and his team prioritize theirs. Because they are on different product teams, their priorities are different. No one has the bandwidth to own components over the long term. These misalignments will not change; they are the price of leveraging this model. It's not until operational improvements are realized from sharing work that companies fund design system teams, hence the constraint.

Revisiting our quote from the beginning of the chapter, Stravinsky wrote, "Whatever diminishes constraint diminishes strength." This may seem counterintuitive. Wouldn't constraints hold you back? Imagine a rushing river. The constraints of its banks contribute to its speed and force. If you take away the banks of the river, you have a marsh. In the design system example, if Bart and Moira try to remove the constraints before they proceed, they would come to a standstill. The constraints are well beyond their control. To shift the constraints, they need to convince leadership from multiple organizations to invest in a program that hasn't yet paid off for the business. By acknowledging the constraints, Bart and Moira can team up, stay close, and drive their shared goal.

In the *Harvard Business Review*, Oguz A. Acar, Murat Tarakci, and Daan van Knippenberg reviewed 145 empirical studies about the effects of constraints on creativity and innovation in an article titled "Why Constraints Are Good for Innovation." They found that "individuals, teams, and organizations alike benefit from a healthy dose of constraints... when there are no constraints on the creative process, complacency sets in, and people follow what psychologists call the path-of-least-resistance—they go for the most intuitive idea that comes to mind rather than investing in the development of better ideas. Constraints, in contrast, provide focus and a creative challenge that motivates people to search for and connect information from different sources to generate novel ideas for new products, services, or business processes."

Bart and Moira embrace the constraints to find a solution to this problem. The first thing they need to do is *understand the situation and each other through outcomes and values*. The problem itself is straightforward. This design system is currently a volunteer effort; there are no team members able to own components. Any one person's focus on items in the design system waxes and wanes, making it unclear how and when work will get done. As Moira and Bart discuss their different teams' outcomes and values, there is a lot of alignment. Both want the best outcomes for their users, including consistency across products for excellent user experiences. And both highly value their teams' time and energy. No one wants to burden their team with work over and above what's already on their plates, which are full.

The big *misalignment* is that Bart and Moira work for different teams. Bart's priorities are his product work, and Moira's priorities are her product work. They see that the design system has created an intersection, and therefore interdependencies, between their teams. At this intersection is work that needs to be done—with no owner, no leader, and no budget. This awareness doesn't solve the problem, but it reduces psychological friction by creating empathy between Bart and Moira. It also clarifies the problem, aiding in reducing cognitive friction.

Several times, I have seen teams in this situation try to solve this type of situation, intentionally or not, by escalating one another until someone wins and someone loses. This is exactly what you do not want to do. Escalation creates threat. It creates winners and losers, and it involves even more people, up the length of the management chain. We don't want to introduce those dynamics of threat and mistrust if we can at all help it, especially when those same people are expected to work together. Rather, we want to empower people with the tools and autonomy to solve their own problems. This is why the next step is to innovate—to find a solution other than the obvious ones on the table. At this point, those are a) fund a design system team, b) add the responsibility to Moira's or Bart's team workload, and c) scrap the concept of a design system altogether. If multiple teams are impacted by the problem, as in this case, it's great to do this work collectively. Multiple points of view provide more and higher quality ideas.

Moira and Bart set aside some time to innovate on this problem using the ideation techniques in the exercises section of this book. Ideation is a way of opening up creativity, challenging traditional thought, and bringing novel ideas to the table. Bart and Moira include developers and designers from other product areas, since this is something that affects everyone. Through the exercise, they come up with several workable ideas:

- Host a monthly design system hackathon where everyone from all teams spends a few days focused completely on updating the design system.

- Hire part-time contractors to work on the design system until there is funding.

- Assign the work to low-paid interns.

- Add buffers in product team budgets to allow for time spent on the design system.

The leadership team was impressed by the different options and selected several. They were entering the third quarter when budgets traditionally go on lockdown, so spending money was not an option. The leadership liked the teamwork inherent in the hackathon idea and supported teams scheduling one every other month until the end of the year. At the same time, multiple leaders committed to adding internship funding to their budgets for the following fiscal year. In the long run, interns could be a long-term, lower-cost addition, which would allow the leaders to fund a smaller design system team, when the time comes.

After only a couple hours of innovation, the team, led by Moira and Bart, was able to provide several possible processes to address the maintenance and growth of the design system. No escalation was necessary, and the leadership leveraged several ideas for the short- and long-term health of the design system and the organization.

Look Forward, Not Backward

Whether you are observing friction within the team or are planning for a significant change, the starting place is the same. It always begins with the question "What does success look like?" and is quickly followed by "How will we know we're headed in that direction?" Avoid the temptation to lean into process too early. Don't be deceived by the illusion of productivity when all you may be doing is moving things around—shift this step over here, add that team to this call, go talk to someone… If you're not achieving your outcome, you need to first validate that everyone sees the same vision and understands their contributions and each other's.

Think of this exercise like a jigsaw puzzle. The picture on the puzzle box is what success looks like. Each piece inside the box is necessary to complete that picture. If even one person is pulling pieces from the wrong box, you're going to have a problem. Agree on what you are doing and what everyone's contributions are. Only then can you start working with the things that help you achieve success: people, their values, and process.

Nothing else should take place until that information is established, to the best of the leadership's ability, and everyone on the team understands what success looks like and how to know they're going in that direction. These answers don't have to be final; as we've discussed, culture continually evolves. But the answers should be concrete enough to keep the team moving forward for three to six months. Unless you are at the beginning of a very major change, culture should not need to be revisited more than once every three months.

My clients are often surprised I do not recommend a detailed examination of what's wrong with the organization and how they got there. Some people find this information helpful when trying to make improvements. I've found that looking backward often leads to assigning blame to a team or individual, which I avoid at all costs. In helping teams define healthy cultures that drive toward business outcomes, not once has value been derived from identifying an individual who made a mistake. Mistakes are made because:

- Outcomes were unclear
- People didn't have the tools or the right judgment to make a better choice
- Values did not align with business outcomes

Your goal is to identify those things, and the right outcomes will follow. Focus on defining the future and building what's necessary to get and stay there *as long as it's serving you.* When it stops serving you, it's time to see where change needs to happen to realign on the new definition of success, close the gaps, and get back to work.

Here's a scenario that shows the difference between looking backward and looking forward. As you read, take note of how you respond emotionally and physically.

The Forward-Looking Approach

Jennifer was the new director of outside sales for a team of forty-five people in the western region of a North American transit company. Jennifer hosted an offsite meeting for her team at a hotel in South Lake Tahoe. Though she'd attended these types of events, it was her first time hosting, and her inexperience showed. The hotel was too small and didn't have the amenities they needed for the meeting to go smoothly. The team experienced issues with almost everything, including the technology and support, catering, and conference room size and temperature, among other things.

Everyone knew the meetings did not go smoothly. Wisely, Jennifer wanted to make sure this did not happen again. In addition to documenting everything she learned, she turned this into an opportunity to define success for next year's offsite. To do this, Jennifer took a forward-looking approach. Together, the team decides that, in a perfect world, at next year's offsite:

- The meeting will run according to the agenda without unexpected interruptions.
- The room will comfortably accommodate everyone.

- Audiovisual needs will be met and include an onsite support contact.

- Everyone on the team will have enough menu options to stay well fed and focused, and there will be food and drinks available throughout the days to keep people energized.

- The room will stay reasonably clean and free from wrappers, soda cans, water bottles, and other debris so people have room to work.

- The meetings will be recorded and scribes assigned to send out notes.

- Days will last no more than eight hours, and scribes will keep people on task with the agenda.

By taking a forward-looking approach, Jennifer and her team can see success. Now all they need to do is reach that definition. This approach naturally leaves behind anything that doesn't need to come forward to reach success. Because Jennifer had never planned an event like this before, she did not consider things outside her subject matter expertise. Things like room size and temperature, technical support, and food service were not even on her radar. Through this exercise, she and her team decided what success should look like, and it's easy enough to reach.

The Backward-Looking Approach
What if Jennifer had led the team through what might be called a postmortem, or a full examination of the situation? These usually conclude with a list of things that went wrong, such as:

- The audiovisual systems did not work for everyone, and it was hard to get timely support from the hotel. We lost time, and the agenda ran over.
- The conference room was too small. There wasn't enough room for people and all their gear.
- Because the room was crowded, it was uncomfortably warm, which made it hard to stay focused.
- The food choices were inadequate for individuals who are vegetarian, vegan, kosher, or gluten free; some people didn't get enough to eat, got cranky, and had trouble maintaining energy.
- Janitorial services didn't clean the room during the course of the day, resulting in trash on the table and overflowing wastebaskets.

There's a difference between mining the past for information to make better decisions in the future and figuring out what went wrong and why. When presented with a list of problems, it's natural for people to ask how those problems arose. Who picked the hotel? Did anyone think to ask attendees about diet restrictions? Did the organizers understand the team's audiovisual and business center needs? I could go on. But the point is the conversation would be going in the wrong direction. It's obvious that mistakes were made, mostly through the absence of information. This fact has been established. Will the answers to these questions help Jennifer's team plan a more successful offsite for the sales team? No, they won't. Instead, they *distract* from building a plan to achieve success, and they assign blame.

You cannot travel back in time to change things. When defining success, look forward to what you want the outcome to be and then set about making that reality. Anything of value from the past will come forward into the new reality you are building, and whatever was not valuable will naturally be left behind.

Relationship Repair Through Trust Building

There is one exception to the rule about looking forward, not backward: *relationships*. If people have been operating in a challenging culture, they might be wounded by a lack of trust or a disbelief that things will actually change. Mona comes to mind. Recall that she and her fellow senior directors did not trust their executive leaders to make a long-term commitment to the organization's transformation. And recall also that Anusha did not trust senior directors to lead their teams through the digital transformation in a timely manner. Repair started in the workshop where Mona's team showed Anusha they could prioritize the common good over the ill will. They were able to communicate their desire for a more dialogue-based relationship with executive leadership. These changes and others led to enhanced alignment and helped repair trust between both parties.

Trust is a critical ingredient in any culture that expects people to thrive. When trust is damaged, it takes demonstrated and consistent changes over time to repair. Once trust is broken, the situation or person who broke it is coded in memory as a threat and can trigger psychological friction; they don't have to say or do anything. This is one of those "can't unsee" moments: once you understand what's happening on a neurological level when trust is threatened, it's impossible to ignore. For the prosperity of the team and the health of the organization, you must seize any opportunity to actively reduce and eliminate situations that feel threatening to you or your teammates. Clean that up immediately.

What does repair look like? In the case of Mona and Anusha, and in any situation where friction exists, it starts with active listening, which is listening to *understand the other person's complete message*. It is not about agreeing or disagreeing. And critically for the listener, it's *not about sharing your point of view*. (There is an active listening exercise in the back of the book.)

It's hard to hear someone say things that upset you or to feel you've been misunderstood. Let's revisit our software squad for a deep example of how active listening played a vital role in repairing cultural friction.

Emma (the senior design manager) had a very vocal style of leadership. Emma wanted Jo (the lead designer) to lead in the same visible way. Emma's expectations did not mesh with Jo's personality, upbringing, or beliefs, despite how many times she told Jo what she expected and how to act like a leader (in Emma's eyes, at least). Emma felt Jo was not up to the task, and Jo felt torn up inside, to the point of wanting to leave. She believed it was disrespectful to defy leadership, but she was being asked to act in a way that was inorganic to who she was. It was impossible for her.

Jo told me, "I understand what Emma's saying, but it's like asking a cat to become a bird." To complicate matters, Emma's way of working required Jo to act in a way that she felt was disrespectful to the executive team. Emma didn't see it that way and told Jo people would respect her more if she stood up and disagreed more often, rather than keeping her opinion to

Space and time need to be made for people to safely share their feelings

herself. Jo felt stuck between two bad options. It's no wonder she wanted to leave.

To address this problem, in a workshop setting, I created a space of active listening. I do this by asking people to answer questions on stickies and then share them with the team, one at a time. There is no response: only listening. By the time we have gone around the room, everyone has had a chance to be heard. Then we move forward by defining success. What do we want to see, hear, and experience at work? And what do we not want to see, hear, and experience?

As you go through this exercise, you learn what people need to feel engaged again. You also discover patterns of what people want and don't want. Sounds pretty easy, right? Do those things, and don't do those other things. Usually people request that cultural shifts be made.

If there's any heavy lifting that comes from this work, it lands on leadership's shoulders because they set the tone. Most often, one or more of the three pillars of culture design is missing or unclear, the leader is lacking soft skills and it's time to level up, or the leader is operating from their own cultural or psychological friction. They may be operating from some past threat-informed point of view; they may have developed a behavior that makes them feel safe and they're projecting that onto others. Or perhaps their feedback is not right for the situation. This is what happened between Emma and Jo.

Throughout Emma's career, she needed to prove herself ad nauseam. Her success came down to showing she was right, and therefore worthy of her role, a promotion, being listened to, recognized for her ideas, and so on. Over twenty years, Emma built up a set of processes that functioned very well for her. She could safely abstract a conversation to the input and output of business processes: if you want business result C, we do A and B. This is a valuable approach, but it is limited to the execution processes, code, designs, testing, and so on. It is not suited for coaching soft skills. If you follow the process, you are doing things right and you get the right result. If you don't follow the process, you get the wrong result. It's rather rigid, but it had served her needs.

Jo, on the other hand, prides herself on building relationships with her cross-functional team members. She invests a great deal of time getting to know people and understanding their organization's outcomes so she can partner with them. She and I often talked about how she was a bit of a chameleon, shapeshifting to fit in, build rapport, and become a trusted partner. Jo got results, but Emma felt Jo wasn't a leader.

Emma was judging Jo's success by how often Jo spoke up in meetings, the tone of her voice, and how often she appeared to "put her foot down." Jo judged success by a very different measure: how deeply her partners trusted her. Emma's and Jo's varying definitions of success became apparent in the workshop, and they both had lightbulb moments discovering their differences. There was no argument, no discussion of right or wrong, leader versus follower. There was simply a decision to make: how is leadership measured in this organization?

The answer to this question impacted everyone because there needed to be continuity and equality across the whole design organization. Melanie (VP of Design) took the question to her peers on the executive team, who discussed it and designed a rubric of leadership behaviors and outcomes expected at Jo's level and above. What felt like a power struggle between Emma and Jo was really a gap in communication regarding leadership outcomes. By taking the time to discuss and identify the issue (less than an hour), Emma and Jo saw they were talking past each other. They were able to let go of the animosity that had been building up because there was now a definition for everyone.

Space and time need to be made for people to safely share their feelings. People who have been hurt need reassurance that the hurtful behavior will not happen again. This process helps remove the perceived threat and the subsequent cognitive friction from their mental lexicon, allowing them to reengage with their full selves. For that to happen, the hurt needs to be heard and understood. There also needs to be agreement about what the future will look like and a commitment to new ways of working. This can be a two-way street—sometimes hurt begets hurt, and everyone has participated in causing wounds. People come from different backgrounds and have complex histories, so it is difficult to predict what might hurt someone. It could be an ill-timed joke, an inadvertent cultural blunder, a power dynamic, or differing needs around communication.

Most of the hurt I have seen—even some significant missteps by people in high places—was repairable when everyone entered the conversation with a sincere intention to repair past hurts and engaged in active listening. People listened to understand and gain empathy, not to explain their behavior or to make others pay debts. There was a genuine desire to heal and create great outcomes together. If you sense repair is needed, bring in a third party whose role is to facilitate the team's culture outcomes. Experienced facilitators help bring the need for self-awareness to light and deliver the necessary information to the appropriate parties.

In the few cases where repair does not take place or trust is not rebuilt, someone has not kept up their end of the bargain. It's a simple equation but not easy for everyone. Engaging in repair requires self-awareness.

As you embark on designing your culture, you want the best possible opportunities for that culture to take root quickly. Don't let constraints slow you down. Leverage them as opportunities for innovation and a means through which your culture can build momentum. When you encounter areas of significant change, define the future, and forge a path in that direction. Leave the past behind you, so you don't inadvertently build a culture of blame. And repair as needed. Repair is needed less and less as you and your teams build your culture for outcomes.

9

Culture Begets Culture

When you ask people about what it is like being part of a great team, what is most striking is the meaningfulness of the experience... Some spend the rest of their lives looking for ways to recapture that spirit.

PETER SENGE

CULTURE IS an ever-evolving force within a group of people that can function to either advance initiatives and outcomes or hinder them. When human factors are at the forefront of designing a culture for outcomes, your chances for success are exponentially greater. Human attitudes, behaviors, motivations, and actions are incredibly powerful sources of energy. We know intuitively that when people are heard, recognized, and included, they operate at a higher level. When they are ignored, overlooked, or taken of advantage of, they either freeze in place, shut down, or leave.

It's painful to think of all the team integrations I experienced where teams played silent games of tug-of-war for power and safety, using things like process, software, file structures, and naming conventions, or bickering about who was or was not invited to meetings or copied on emails that dispensed critical knowledge. Finding synergies and evaluating misalignments is a fail-safe method for eliminating common power struggles. When you have the tools to avoid this kind of situation from occurring altogether, it can take only a few days to a few weeks for culture change to set in. Culture begets culture, in whichever direction it is heading.

The Squad Six Months Out

It's only fitting that we should end where we began: with our software squad. I'd like to dive a little deeper into the work we did to turn their ship around, beyond what I've already shared with you. Recall the players on this team are:

The Doers	The Executives
Carlos: Engineering architect	Carol: VP of Software
Jiang: Lead developer	Ethan: Chief technology officer
Mei: Product owner	Barry: VP of Product
Jeffrey: Senior designer	Melanie: VP of Design
Jo: Lead designer	Emma: Senior design manager
Arun: Early career designer	

Within six months of the design team's culture work, the squad's mission expanded twice. Both expansions included integrating additional people into the team. Some of those people did the same kind of work the squad was doing, and some people did different kinds of work. The squad was working on a particularly critical project for the hotel—functionality that promised to pave the way for the future of the organization—so it made sense that other teams would integrate with them and not the other way around.

In the early stages of the integration, the incoming team members struggled with fear and anxiety. During regular follow-up consultations with the squad's leadership, we identified what most worried these new members was their roles. Remember how identity is often tied to the value someone believes they bring to a project, team, or organization?

Armed with this information, the software squad was able to calm the incoming team members' anxiety and *reduce their psychological and cognitive friction* by preserving their identities as valuable subject matter experts who would continue to be integral to the project's success. This wasn't accomplished with words alone. The different teams spent several days together aligning visions, outcomes, terminology, and finally processes. Clarity emerged, and people's roles started to fall into place. It became clear how most people were to contribute, and their identities were preserved.

The squad and its new members avoided weeks, if not months, of slowdowns caused by the cognitive, cultural, and psychological friction that comes from wandering through invisible mazes of human needs. Jeffrey, Carlos, Mei, and the rest of the squad had developed a culture of safety and trust, built on a scaffolding of intentional communication and guided by retrospectives that naturally drew out and solved potential friction points among their new peers *before friction entered the system*. The way retrospectives were conducted, along with a contract for change, showed incoming team members what was valued, how conflict was handled, how the team held itself accountable, and other behavioral norms. This transparency and intentionality kept friction down and increased trust.

Since people felt safe and valued and they understood the vision and outcomes, collaboration increased, and knowledge and creativity flowed swiftly between team members. Over time, Ethan, Barry, and even Carol noticed a real change in the team and the ideas they were bringing forward. It seemed the original innovation squad had burst its creative seams!

The executive team complimented Carlos, Jeffrey, Mei, and Jo on their leadership and the rest of the team on their innovation. The moment of executive alignment used to start when the senior executives saw concepts for the first time. The concepts sparked executives' imaginations in ways they couldn't experience on their own, kicking off discussions that should have happened weeks earlier. Now the team came to the table with ideas so well formed and even tested with users that they served to align the executives.

The team experienced a new level of influence on customer outcomes, which impacted business outcomes. For Jeffrey, Jo, and Arun, this was the place they longed to be. They were now able to bring their expertise in human factors and design into the project earlier. They performed user research to help Carlos, Mei, and Jiang understand the outcomes customers wanted and what would build the customer relationships Carol was counting on.

Designing the necessary culture to facilitate the working style and communications structures they needed, and to scale this, reduced friction points. It also improved and sped up trust building across teams as they joined the organization. All this critical groundwork improved operational efficiency, reduced costs, and improved quality because there were fewer misunderstandings as well as less churn in the system. With a lot of negative influences gone and positive influences amplified, the team had the time and safety to be creative. They were able to collaborate, run through more ideas, and mature ideas faster.

A key ingredient in the successful integration of the original squad with the others, and the business outcomes experienced by the larger team, was that the original squad had intentionally done the work to develop their culture. That culture served as a foundation, which functioned first by presenting clear values for the new members. Second, the methodology of starting with vision, purpose, and values set a precedent for discussing changes to the team culture that new members found necessary. The clarity of culture allowed the squad to amplify it and to blend with the needs of incoming teammates.

The software squad did not need to redo the whole process when new team members joined the organization, though that was certainly an option. Nor did they need to announce "We value transparency!" or "We value protected space for the kind of creative endeavors upon which our business outcomes rely!" No one would ever say such a thing. But they *did* protect their creative space by going dark on instant messaging and blocking their calendars. They *did* honor the creative space of their colleagues. They *did* drive constructive feedback and avoid negative feelings in meetings by approaching one another with curiosity. They *did* document their work so others could see how things were done. They *did* feel safe to escalate to Emma and Melanie when they were pressured to work through the weekend because Ethan and Barry did not meet to align. As a result, requirements were clarified at 3 p.m. on a Wednesday afternoon, and they were reviewed with Carol at 1 p.m. the following Monday. These commitments, and more like them, *demonstrate* the culture. When culture is easy to understand and facilitates business outcomes, people thrive.

Culture change did not stop there. A critical shift happened as an outcome of the teams merging in this way, which added gravitas to the team's point of view: power structures were balanced. Remember, the executive team had crept into the daily operations of the squad because of a lack of outcomes. This meant that the squad had been overpowered by executives, which wasn't helpful because it was out of dysfunction. The team had no way to push back.

With others merging into the innovation squad, the team enlarged, and the healthy culture expanded. This led to better collaboration between disciplines. What was originally a team of fifteen doers being pulled between their need to work together and executive misalignment had become a team of roughly thirty-five doers moving through the ocean of uncertainty like a school of fish. Together, they had become an organism large enough to take up space and cast a shadow in the water. They were banded together by values and a vision that exceeded the feature ideas any executive had been driving. More than balancing the power of the executive ranks, the orchestration and coordination with which they worked and presented their ideas was in stark contrast to the executive misalignment. It made this misalignment clear without anyone having to say anything, and it did so through a cross-functional team aligned on customer outcomes and the conditions the team needed to execute those outcomes.

This would not have happened if the team's output had been mediocre. It's very important to recognize that the culture spread because it generated outcomes. People wanted more of this secret sauce that increased innovation and reduced operational costs and defects. Because the team had created an environment in which everyone's contributions were clear and supported, they worked as more than the sum of their parts. Everyone's visibility increased, which helped underscore to the integrating team members that their professional identities were intact and their contributions valuable.

Imagine what might have happened if the integration had gone the other way—if the squad, who had so intentionally designed their culture, had been integrated into a team that had not already done so. The cognitive, cultural, and psychological friction caused by such a dramatic change could have easily taken over. This would have been compounded by the squad losing the culture they knew helped them do their best work, having it replaced by who knows what.

Fortunately, this scenario did not happen. The original squad had built a foundation of psychological safety by valuing everyone's needs, and they organically assumed the new team members' needs into their retrospectives. We understand how the brain responds under threat, what creates a sense of threat, and how negative bias can take over when left unchecked; hopefully you can understand why I said negative culture can snowball and become toxic. And now you can see that when you intentionally design your culture and put in some simple mechanisms to keep it current as your business changes, positive culture begets more positive culture.

CONCLUSION

Be Inspired

My hope is this book has given you the ability to see more of the inner workings of those around you: as individuals, teams, and organizations. People are the heart of your business. With any luck, you see how providing for them and encouraging them to provide for one another by creating the conditions in which they can thrive is not a heavy lift. It takes creating a continuous thread that connects business outcomes to each individual's purpose and the team's values. Doing this work dramatically reduces, or completely removes, many barriers that create cognitive, cultural, and psychological friction and can lead to toxic cultures.

Wherever you are in your organization, I hope you feel empowered and equipped to start a conversation with your colleagues. To facilitate this, please devote your time and attention to the exercises at the back of the book, which are shared for the sole purpose of helping you design a culture for outcomes—I think you'll find that change is easier than you think. As people experience the ease of working in a culture designed for their business outcomes, they will commit to it and advocate for it.

Let this be the start of the conversation. I invite you into the dream of building a future of frictionless organizations. The map is in your hands.

EXERCISES

Fourteen Activities for Culture Change

The beginning of wisdom is wonder.
SOCRATES

WE KNOW CHANGE HAPPENS from the inside out. To facilitate a sense of agency and ownership among individuals, teams, and companies, I've put together some of my favorite and most effective exercises to help jump-start designing your culture. Though you will gain important insights by doing these exercises individually, in pairs, or in small groups, for the full effect, you will want to do them in a workshop setting at the team, the organization, or the company-wide leadership level. A trained facilitator or external consultant is highly recommended. You might pass these exercises along to others on your team as a warm-up for a full workshop. Each exercise is also effective on its own, so go ahead and jump in! You will quickly get the feel for how these exercises shed light on both friction and opportunity.

The exercises are arranged in the order I recommend you approach them, especially if you are doing them for the first time. The first three exercises—hopes and fears, empathy map, and active listening—help prepare for the work you are about to do. The So That method, So That cascade, business impact worksheet, and future impact article help you ensure you are building on the solid foundation of business outcomes and vision. The team purpose, people vision, values, and contract for change are where you do the work of defining and committing to your culture. The last exercises—doable versus valuable, contrarian thinking, and ideation—are supportive exercises to use if you get stuck.

If you've done any design thinking, some of these exercises will feel familiar. Design thinking is a set of tools and exercises for understanding problem or opportunity spaces and innovating solutions. Some of these exercises are design thinking activities that I've repurposed for culture design, and some of these exercises I designed. When you and your colleagues explore these exercises and gather to share your discoveries, you will learn about hidden misalignments, assumptions, motivations, and opportunities.

The Benefits of "Working at the Wall"

As you move through these exercises, the first thing you will notice is that most of them are done using sticky notes. Traditionally, this is done by drawing or printing templates onto 25-by-30-inch paper and hanging them on the wall. People then answer prompts on 3-by-3-inch sticky notes and place them on the template, resulting in a colorful collage that captures all the participants' thoughts. This is referred to as "working at the wall." You may also use a virtual wall like Miro,

Mural, or even a spreadsheet or document to track ideas. I don't favor documents and spreadsheets as they don't facilitate the interconnectedness of ideas and the relationships throughout the system. Your team or organization is a system of interlocking parts (individuals, departments, tools, and technology) that influence each other. The more often you can maintain a visible reminder of your interrelatedness during these exercises, the more accurate and effective your work will be, and the better your outcomes.

Another potential drawback to spreadsheets and documents is that people can perceive the information in these formats as prioritized lists when the real goal of this work is to facilitate understanding of the system as a whole. Having said that, most document and spreadsheet software is accessible to users with disabilities, and inclusion is the most important factor.

Working at the wall with ideas applies to the following exercises:

- Hopes and fears
- Empathy map
- Team purpose
- People vision
- Values
- Doable versus valuable
- Contrarian thinking
- Ideation

These exercises act at the intersections of business outcomes and human beings—that place where values and friction influence behavior, and behavior becomes outcomes. When you work at the wall, you can see what patterns, synergies, and conflicts emerge from parts of the system, as well as how those things affect the system over time.

In addition to taking a holistic view, working at the wall means ideas persist. You are making decisions on data from the whole system, not on people's short-term memories, whatever was said last, or what was said by the highest-ranking person in the room. Everyone's ideas need to be considered for two reasons: because they are people, and because they are influencing or being influenced by the system.

What you *don't* want to do is optimize for one person, team, or organization at the expense of another—especially if the collateral damage is unexpected and shows up later as friction. There will be moments when it seems you are at odds with one another. A typical response is to interpret the situation as a false dichotomy and play tug-of-war with ideas. When dichotomies appear, they are usually the result of limited thinking, or people wanting to get out of a difficult situation by forcing an answer—any answer. I don't think dichotomies happen very often in complex systems like those that make up organizations. There's always a lever to pull for change; it may just take some creativity. That's where the exercises at the end—contrarian thinking and ideation—will be helpful for you. When you feel stuck, step back, take a break, and when you return, give your minds a good airing out with one of those two exercises. Sometimes tradeoffs need to be made to get to a solution. Situations may not offer great options for everyone all the time; what you want is choice so you can act and make tradeoffs *with intention*.

Working at the wall using the methods in this book will help you mitigate risks. With all the information on the table, you can go in search of how best to fit everyone together to achieve some shared goal or outcome. This is why we start with outcomes and work backward. If you don't have shared outcomes, you are no longer a system but a collection of unrelated parts.

The last point to make about working at the wall is the sense of teaming. When all the data are on a wall on one side of the physical or virtual room and all the people are on the other side, there is less potential to hold on to one's own idea. At the wall, ideas are typically anonymous. This dynamic allows the ideas to take on lives of their own, each worthy of consideration. Through this, everyone aligns on what is important to achieve the outcomes. This alignment can quickly build additional layers of camaraderie throughout your team. You may be delighted by how the politics seem to drain out of the room through the workshopping dynamics created by taking such a holistic approach.

Working with Ideas

The overarching method for this work is to gather people's thoughts on topics, whether it's just yours or your team's, and then to reflect on those thoughts by taking certain things into consideration. This iterative ideation work is about revealing and identifying. In a workshop, you will not stop to solve problems—understanding and solving are two different activities and you want to keep momentum going in your workshops. You will take action items and pull together task forces to address problems after your workshop. If you are pulling out an exercise or two to use for the sole purpose of understanding a specific problem, then of course keep going.

To track ideas, these exercises call for individuals to write their ideas on stickies or in spreadsheets or documents. As you do this, keep the following in mind:

- The size of stickies—3-by-3-inch—is recommended for a reason. We are working with thoughts and ideas, and we want to just get the idea out. Don't worry about how it might be executed, any politics that might get in the way, or if others will agree. This work is not intended to stand on its own like a presentation. Ideas are there to facilitate discussion. As facilitator, you will be present to ensure there are no misunderstandings. When working with spreadsheets or documents, the same applies. You may need to be extra conscious of this because you won't have the size constraint of a sticky as a reminder.
- Keep yourself to one idea per sticky, or one idea per row if using spreadsheets or documents. You will be moving ideas around, so they need to be separate from one another.
- At times, you may be guessing at ideas. For example, if you are doing an empathy map for someone new to you, you will be guessing what they are thinking. Put question marks in the corners of those stickies so you remember to validate them. Agree on a way to annotate spreadsheets and documents, so you know where the assumptions are.

The Flow

The exercises in the bulleted list in The Benefits of "Working at the Wall" all follow the same general flow, with exceptions noted in the instructions for specific exercises:

1. Write down ideas, either as individuals or teams
2. Prune ideas to the top two or three

3   Read ideas out to the group as you go

4   Mine the wall for information and value

5   Discuss and reflect

Write Your Ideas
Each exercise will give you either a single question or a series of questions. Using the guidance under Working with Ideas, write down your answers, one per sticky (or one per line in a document or spreadsheet). Keep it simple: just the what, not the how.

Prune Your Ideas
Some facilitators run several rounds of prioritization exercises as a means of pruning down ideas. My preference is for people to practice their own prioritization, sensing what is most important to them and letting go of the rest. I still want you to write down all your ideas; you can't choose the most important ones until you've captured them. Filtering ideas in your head as you go consumes your executive function, the mental skills required for working memory, cognitive flexibility, and emotional management. So have all your great ideas, then prioritize where you want to focus. Those are the ideas you will bring forward. When working as a team, you will first answer questions as individuals, then combine and synthesize everyone's answers together. From there, you will choose the top two or three answers.

Read Out and Group
The readout flow is the same for both individual- and team-level work. When it comes time for the readout, use the following process to group ideas as you go. It is a more

streamlined approach than every person or team reading out every single answer and then grouping.

1. The first person or team places their answers in the template and reads out their ideas. For a team, choose a spokesperson to read the group's stickies.

2. The first person/team pauses after each answer so the rest of the participants can consider their answers. Anyone with a similar answer places their sticky in the same area of the template, to form a cluster of like answers. Answers don't need to be identical, but they should be close enough that people can see the similarities.

3. Add a descriptive label to the cluster of answers.

4. The person or team continues on until all of their answers have been read. The next group then reads out their remaining answers, following the same flow. Do this until all answers have been read.

There are several ways to follow this flow when using a spreadsheet or document. Everyone can work on paper, then follow the process above, adding their top two to three answers to the spreadsheet or document as answers are read out. Another option is for everyone to add their answers to the spreadsheet or document and then spend some time copying and pasting answers so similar answers are near each other; once that's done, add a descriptive label at the top of each answer group.

Don't worry if you have stand-alone stickies or ideas that don't fit into a group—what I call outliers. They are no less important. Depending on the prompt or question asked, the number of answers in a group might be irrelevant. A single novel idea might be the innovation the organization needs to jump-start its next chapter; I've seen that happen over and over again. The most important part of a readout is to actively listen to understand each other.

Mining Your Ideas

In several of the exercises, you will mine your ideas for specific things: synergies, overlaps, divergences, and gaps. This is a great practice to hone and use any time you are looking at your business processes. You really start to see how your system is functioning. For some exercises, this overview is enough. If additional nuance is needed, you will find that in the instructions for that particular exercise.

- **Synergies** are when multiple people or teams are working in the same area, perhaps making different contributions, toward outcomes that transcend the outcome of any one team. Make sure everyone is clear on how these areas are synergistic. When you find synergies, place an S in the corner of the stickies involved (or next to the item in the spreadsheet or document). Take an action item to discuss later, and make sure that action item has an owner who will drive it. When you get to solutioning, you want to ask yourselves how things would be different if this synergy reached its maximum potential. You may want to leverage the ideation, the business impact worksheet, or people vision exercises to explore the synergies.

- **Overlaps** occur when two teams have very similar or identical answers to a question. True overlaps are wasteful because two teams are doing the same thing, and one's time could be repurposed. True overlaps can also cause friction among teams because both teams think they own a task or outcome when really one of them is better positioned or qualified. When left unaddressed, friction arises. Go back and read the situation between Carlos and Jeffrey in the Psychological Friction section of Chapter 4 for an example of two people who feel responsible for the same tasks and what happens to morale when that friction is not addressed.

Using the So That approach is a great way to help clarify if there really is an overlap, or if there are nuances that make the work synergistic between the two teams. If it truly is duplicative, mark it with an O, either on the sticky or in the spreadsheet or document. Then take an action item for a later date to discuss how the overlap is problematic or wasteful and how to resolve the overlap. Make sure that action item has an owner to drive it through.

- **Divergences** are areas where the way people work appear to be pulling teams or people in different directions. This was the case with Bart, Moira, and the design system (see Chapter 8). When their teams operated independently on their own timelines, everything was fine. Then design system components were introduced, creating an interconnectedness. On paper, there was a common goal, but no one had adjusted people's outcomes or processes. Because of this, everyone's main goal was still their own work—everyone was pointing away from common components toward their own deliverables.

   In complex systems made of subsystems (like Bart's team and Moira's team), it is natural to protect your own outcomes and goals. The consequence is that another team is pulled off balance, or friction is introduced through an unexpected new responsibility, conflicting timelines, or outcomes that don't fit together.

These divergences are the opportunities you are mining for and when you find them, note them with a D. Take an action item to discuss the divergence and the friction it causes, and make sure that action item has an owner. Then discuss ways to handle the divergence so the friction is minimized or eliminated. Ideation is a great tool for this.

- **Gaps** are places where something should be taking place (a task, communication, a handoff, etc.) but is not. Gaps are simple to address. Gaps might not be represented by a sticky or a line in a spreadsheet or document. They may only be identified by the problem caused in their absence. In these cases, add a sticky (or line in a spreadsheet or document), label it G, and write down the gap and its consequence. Then take an action item to close the gap. Make sure that action item has an owner to drive it.

Discuss and Reflect

In this last phase, you want to reflect on your work and add any final notations, action items, questions, and assumptions. Make sure that everything is documented either at the wall or in spreadsheets and documents. Make sure you have all your symbols (S, O, D, G, and ?) present to represent everything you discovered during your mining phase. Check that the action items are clear and each has an owner. Lastly, if working at a physical wall, take photos of all the stickies on the templates and share them in a central location so everyone present has access to this excellent system knowledge. If working with documents or spreadsheets, make sure everyone has access.

Exercise 1: Hopes and Fears

What It Is
Do this exercise so that you can uncover your aspirations, which often include some aspect of motivation, and your fears, which can trigger friction and slow you down. When you write things down, you can see them. When you can see them, you can figure out how to act (if you want to act) on these things. Documenting your hopes and fears provides a level of agency by naming the thing versus sensing a vague blob of "ugh" or "yippee" or both. When done as a group exercise, you can see where the team is trending. This visibility allows you to get ahead of problem areas or avoid them altogether.

When to Use It
My favorite times to use this exercise are:

- Before launching a new initiative to get a sense of where negative emotions are arising—warning: friction ahead!

- When you are experiencing negative feelings and need to figure out what is causing them

- To mine far-reaching or aspirational aspects of a successful outcome (from the hopes section)

- To understand what leadership can do to support the team, mitigate fears, and increase the potential for hopes

How to Do It
- Create your hopes and fears template as in the diagram.

- Write down your hopes and fears, one per sticky note. You can go back and forth between the two, as they come to mind.

- Read out according to the directions in The Flow section.

- Step back and look for patterns. Do any of your fears point to a deeper concern? Are there cause-and-effect relationships among your responses? Group those together in a cluster and give the cluster a descriptive label.

- Decide what action(s) you want to take and when. Consider who you could partner with for support to decrease the negative or to amplify the positive.

HOPES	FEARS

HOPES

Collaboration

- We will become more collaborative
- Collaboration will go all the way up to the executive level
- We will break down the silos

Alignment

- Our OKRs will be related across silos
- We will have dept. visions that fit together
- We will be able to prioritize in coordination with each other

Operational improvement

- We will find ways to be more efficient/save money
- Close process gaps
- Remove process overlaps/duplication
- Everyone will be able to do their jobs well (time, resources, etc.)

Single ideas

- Inspire people to be great and exceed financial expectations
- We will unlock innovation opportunities

Customer focus

- We will have a renewed focus on the customer
- Prioritize customer needs over internal politics
- We will agree on the definition of success for our customers

FEARS

Psychological safety

- This won't be a safe place to tell the truth
- If I speak up about changes I want, I will be a target

Self-reflection

- Some people lack introspection
- People won't be honest with themselves

Misalignment

- Siloed ways of working will get in our way of a good outcome
- Only most powerful group/dept. will be heard
- Stakeholders in each silo will value their own contributors over the bigger picture

Leadership support

- Leaders won't do their part and be held to old standards
- This is just to make us feel good; no sincere intentions to enact change
- Leaders won't support us
- No courage to cancel projects that don't align with new outcomes

False dichotomy

- Seeing financial success and a great place for people, instead of one another
- Reaching for money over caring for people

Customer success

- Prioritizing our own success metrics over those of our customers
- Won't be able to agree on what success means for customers

Exercise 2: Empathy Map

What It Is

Use empathy maps so that you can better understand a person's experience in a situation. The context can be as granular as a single step of a business process or as high level as one's sentiments about showing up to work. I like to think of the empathy map as an exercise in humility. You are setting yourself aside to move into the experience of another person with the goal of understanding them better. Learning about the other person is half the exercise. The other half is cementing in your heart and mind that you cannot possibly know the thoughts or feelings of another. With the exception of observational data, everything about their experience is an assumption on your part. Using an empathy map to understand each other is an excellent way to root out assumptions and identify misunderstandings.

In the middle of the empathy map template is a subject, or the person you are learning more about. The space around the subject is broken into quadrants, Says and Does on one side, Thinks and Feels on the other. Notice that one side is observational. You can hear what the subject says and see what they do. The other side is internal. You cannot see or know what they are feeling or thinking. You might get a sense of how the subject is feeling by observing facial expressions or actions, but there's no guarantee your interpretation is correct. This is where a lot of assumptions happen, which lead to misunderstandings. Think back to Emma and Jo (Chapter 1): misunderstandings abounding!

When completed, you have a better understanding of how someone is responding to or engaging with a situation. An empathy map is a great way to remember that the subject is a human being with their own context formed by their experiences. Until you enter a dialogue with this person, you only know what you see, but you don't know why or what it means to them. An empathy map helps you get a fuller picture.

When to Use It

Use the empathy map whenever you want to understand someone better or want them to understand you better—whether it's someone you know or think you know, or someone you're working with for the first time. I recommend empathy maps in the following situations:

- There is friction between people, either inter- or intra-team. Use an empathy map to understand what's going on inside people, draw out pain points, and reveal assumptions. In this case, people would complete their own empathy map to share with others.

- Someone new enters the team, whether as a doer or a leader. I ask my new hires to meet with all their cross-functional partners and have them fill out empathy maps and discuss them. This helps people learn how everyone ticks.

- During or after a challenging situation. Use an empathy map to understand what feelings and thoughts might be lurking in the background that could use repair. You may also spot behavior changes (in the Does quadrant) that resulted from the challenge. You can evaluate those changes to see if they are positive or indicate the need for repair.

- To better understand someone you find difficult to work with. Empathy helps humanize someone who has become a threat. Understanding someone doesn't mean they've changed, but you're seeing them as a human being in the context of a problematic situation. That can bring them back down to size and allow you to reclaim your agency. Often a person exhibiting threatening behavior is ignorant of their impact or is in their own hyperarousal. When made aware of this, people usually choose to change. No one wants to be "that person," the bad apple poisoning the whole bunch.

How to Do It

- Choose a person you want to understand better and the context in which they are working. The example in the completed template uses the scenario from Chapter 7 of Soo and the spreadsheet.

- In the center of the map, write the person's name, context, and doodle a little sketch of the person. You don't need to be an artist: just add a couple of eyes, a nose, a mouth, and maybe some hair. This serves as a gentle reminder that this is a human being we're talking about.

- Write down your ideas, spending some time in each quadrant. Within each quadrant, document your observations and thoughts. Feel free to move between quadrants as insights come to you; you don't need to work in any particular order. In this exercise, you are not limited to two or three ideas. Generate as many as you can.

SAYS

- My team is 4% the size of others
- Team, document all positive outcomes
- I can't lose anyone

THINKS

- This is bad for business
- At odds with my values
- Can I trust my peers?

DOES

- Researches how to demonstrate outcomes
- Has a heart-to-heart with her manager
- Talks to mentors about better ways to handle layoffs

FEELS

- Angry—process is unfair
- Scared—could lose my job
- Courageous—I have integrity

SOO MANAGER

Helpful Hints

While doing empathy maps, people often confuse thoughts for feelings. Many times, in the Feels quadrant, I have seen stickies with a phrase such as "Why can't Jo just do what I say?" or "Why does Jeffrey question my approach?" Those types of observations belong in the Thinks or Says quadrant. You can then ask yourself what someone might be feeling as they uttered or thought the phrase. Frustrated. Angry. Anxious. Those are the types of observations that go into the Feels quadrant.

Many people have a hard time discerning or naming feelings. When this occurs, I use a feeling wheel. (A quick Internet search will bring up something magical, especially helpful for the neuro-diverse.) A feeling wheel is a series of concentric circles that help people get more precise about naming their feelings. The inside circle contains the main categories of feelings: happy, sad, scared, angry, etc. The next concentric circle out is another level of nuance. Most wheels I've seen come in two or three levels of feelings.

- We know there will be guesses and assumptions. Make note of them as you go by drawing a question mark in the corner, or circle back and note them when the exercise is complete. Getting those questions answered will bring you into alignment with your subject and help you better understand them.

- Step back and reflect. Sometimes this exercise can be biased toward the negative. Review for that, and make sure you didn't miss anything.

- Note any gaps. What information do you want that you don't have? How will it help you?

- Sit quietly and allow yourself to empathize with your subject. Note down any thoughts or feelings you have. Are there changes you want to make in how you work? Questions to be answered? Ideas about working together better or differently?

- Decide how and when you will act on this information, which would include reviewing the empathy map with the subject to get corrections or spark a discussion.

Exercise 3: Active Listening

What It Is

Active listening is a great tool to use in conjunction with empathy maps if you are able to dialogue with the subject of your map. Active listening is listening to understand, not to respond. Your role as the listener is to reflect on what you hear and be changed by it as much as is needed to understand. Active listening is about the other person being heard and having their point of view mirrored back to them as a means of validating they have been heard correctly. If not, they get a chance to restate what they said until the listener does understand. Again, the goal here is to understand. When in listening mode, you are not in a position to approve, disapprove, or weigh in on someone's experience in any way. When in speaker mode, you are not trying to convince someone that you are right and they are wrong. People's experiences are valid. Active listening is a way of making sure we understand each other.

When to Use It
Always.

How to Do It

- Using "I statements" (examples below), one person communicates their need, hurt, point of view, or whatever the case may be, while the other listens. The speaker should take care to be concise. This should not take longer than two to three minutes per issue. The listener is not to interrupt the speaker. If the listener has a question, they should make a note of it.

- When the speaker is done, the listener responds by restating for the speaker, in their own words, what they heard and understood. It's helpful to reverse the I statement.

- The speaker then makes any corrections to the listener's restatement.

- The listener repeats them.

- The listener may now ask clarifying questions. This is not a dialogue about the issue. It is an opportunity to clarify any ambiguities.

- Now, reverse roles and run the process through again.

Examples of I Statements

Emma: *When I* give you direction and you don't take it, *it makes me feel* ineffective and like you don't respect me or my experience. My job is to see that things get done, but I don't know what to do when you ignore me. *This makes me feel* frustrated because if I cannot see your leadership, I cannot report your success to Melanie.

Jo: *When I* am asked to work in a way that goes against my nature, *it makes me feel like* I'm in the wrong job. *I feel* vulnerable and fear I might be fired. *That* frustrates *me* because I consistently achieve business outcomes, and I don't understand why reporting those business outcomes to Melanie doesn't demonstrate success and leadership. It's just a different kind of leadership.

By talking about yourself, you communicate your own experience instead of placing blame. Whatever your role and wherever you sit in the hierarchy, you are allowed to set boundaries for yourself. Boundaries are not about requiring someone to behave a certain way; they are about clearly communicating what you will and will not accept. If Jo and Emma could not come to an understanding, one of them would likely have left. I statements are a healthy way to communicate boundaries and tolerances without anyone feeling threatened. After all, a boundary is about the person setting the boundary and how they need to be treated; it is not a statement about the other person (though the other person may not like it). This is not just a tool for repair; it's a great way to ensure everyone in the room is heard and understood.

Exercise 4: So That Method

What It Is

So That is a method for identifying outcomes. For example, the customer outcome is the change that happens for a customer as a result of using your product or service. Your business outcomes should be built on the customer outcomes. (Refer to Chapter 2 for detailed examples.) If you are challenged to complete the So That method, you may want to first do the business impact worksheet and then come back to this exercise.

When to Use It

Use the So That method any time you need to validate why you are doing something and what success looks like.

How to Do It

Complete this template:

> We will provide [person / people] with [product / feature / service] so that [outcome for your customer or your business—whichever you're working on at the moment].
>
> **Person / people:** This is the target customer. If you're chasing multiple demographics, you'll define an outcome for each. You may want to go so far as to build personas, which will help you understand the unique needs and motivations of each demographic.
>
> **Product / feature / service:** This is the thing you put into the world to make a difference in people's lives.
>
> **Outcome:** This is not the completion of a task; it is the change that ensues during or after an event. If you are working on a customer outcome, this is the change that happens for the customer. If you are working on your business outcomes, think beyond revenue.

If working with teams of people, senior executives should provide the top-level So That statement. Then they should have other teams write their own to communicate what they expect to contribute to the overarching outcomes.

Exercise 5: So That Cascade

What It Is

In this activity, I want to show you what it looks like when teams organize around So That statements. The main statement is the overarching goal for the project. Each team or discipline, depending on how you are organized, will make different contributions to the overall outcome, and that is where the cascade comes in. Each team lists out their contributions to reaching the overall outcome. Depending on the size and complexity of the project, you may want to add a second layer to your So That statements, called sub-statements, placed between the main statement and the team-level contribution cascade. This is not a complete list of tasks or objectives; the cascade helps teams set direction. You want to make sure teams:

- Are all pointing in the right direction
- Can spot unintended overlaps or gaps
- Are looking at their contributions from the same relative level of fidelity—we don't want one team in the weeds and another team at 30,000 feet

When to Use It

All the time! (I used it a ton as I wrote this book.) As you kick off projects, this exercise serves as an orienting force for the whole team, allowing everyone to clearly understand their role and contribution to the overarching outcome. Over time, especially for large projects that take multiple releases to market, revisit the main So That statement to see if it needs updating, and then update the cascading statements.

The subject for the example of the So That cascade is our Always Home Hotels software squad. If they had started with this exercise, the design team would have been able to position themselves as key players much earlier in the process. Leadership would have been able to align, saving the team from heartache, as well as wasted money and time.

How to Do It

Using the main statement, teams or individual disciplines (depending on how you are organized) list what they can contribute to the main statement. Your team may make more than one contribution to the main statement. Your team may also contribute to multiple sub-statements.

Using our software squad example, these cascades will give you an idea of how the exercise works. Much of the So That statements consist of alignment and research activities. So That statements can take a back seat once there is alignment across teams. You will also notice that a few of these have two So That statements in one!

> **Always Home's main So That statement**
>
> Always Home will provide customers ages twenty-five to thirty-five with personalized recommendations of hotel amenities, local restaurants, and events *so that they have a more convenient, enriched experience, a more delightful stay, and feel Always Home Hotels understands them.*

Cascade to Design Team (Jeffrey, Jo, and Arun; agreed to by Emma and Melanie)

- The design team will conduct research on the customers ages twenty-five to thirty-five, so the team can define exactly what "a more convenient, enriched experience, and a more delightful stay" means to this demographic and what will make them feel like "Always Home Hotels understands them" *so that they and the rest of the team can define exactly what to build to reach the customer outcome and how to measure success.*

- The design team will leverage the outcomes of the research to educate their cross-functional partners and executive leadership and contribute to workshops *so that everyone is current on the needs and experiences of the demographic, so that the cross-functional team defines the features and services that will reach the outcomes.*

- The design team will share the research and workshop outcomes with their cross-functional teammates and executive leadership as a means of alignment *so that everyone is aligned on the outcomes, how the team will achieve them, and how to measure success.*

Cascade to Product Owner (Mei, agreed to by Barry)

- The product team will conduct competitive research *so that they ensure the concepts developed surpass what exists in the market today.* (They are not in the business of parity.)

- The product team will develop a set of metrics to measure the success of the products and services delivered, including direct customer feedback and telemetry gathered through other means, *so that the team can immediately pivot where necessary and persist what works.*

- Recognizing that "a more convenient, enriched experience, a more delightful stay, and feel Always Home Hotels understands them" is being newly defined for this demographic, and that reaching these goals will require participation of other parts of the company, the product team, partnering with Design, will reach out to the Customer Success, Hotel Operations, and the Marketing and Communications departments to update them on the research and the projects *so that all these organizations work in lockstep with the new experiences the team will bring to market, so that the demographic of twenty-five to thirty-five has a consistent, relatable end-to-end brand experience.*

Cascade to Engineering (Carlos and Jiang, agreed to by Ethan)

- Engineering will conduct technical research on available data sources for purchase, the technical cost of integration, and the impact on company experience (like response time, etc.) *so that engineering can provide the rest of the team with viable data options.*

- Engineering will conduct competitive technical research *so that they ensure the concepts developed surpass what exists in the market today.*

- Engineering will conduct technical research on available AI methods and their cost (technical, competitive impact, time) versus building in-house, *so that engineering can provide the most technical power possible to the project, and so that the product owners and designers can best meet the customer outcomes* ("a more convenient, enriched experience, a more delightful stay, and feel Always Home Hotels understands them") *at the lowest cost and get to market as quickly as possible.*

I recommend you do this work with stickies or in collaboration software that allows you to move things around. You may find dependencies throughout the cascade and want to reorder the work accordingly. You may also find areas where teams should be working together or may be duplicating efforts.

Exercise 6: Business Impact Worksheet

What It Is
The business impact worksheet is used when developing and aligning on an organizational vision. Using this exercise and its companion exercise, future impact article, you will develop a vision that leverages the contributions and wisdom of the different disciplines throughout the organization.

The business impact worksheet helps you imagine how embodying your organization's vision might change your overall landscape. If the market, your industry, your company, and your team are not changed by moving the needle on your vision, it may not be big enough.

When to Use It
Use this exercise:

- As a tool to help you establish an organizational vision.

- As a way of checking to see if your vision is visionary enough, or if you need to think a bit bigger.

- To refresh your vision when market or industry conditions change.

- Any time you need to gauge team alignment. It is very interesting to send this worksheet out to entire teams and see what comes back as single teams can be all over the map.

- When you want to mine for new disruptions. Again, send this out to the whole team to see what different impacts people imagine.

How to Do It

In the following instructions, the term "leader" is a bit ambiguous; the answer depends on both how you are organized and the level at which you are doing the work. If working at the C-suite level, the term "leader" applies to the C-suite and probably the senior vice presidents. However, those different levels could gather the contributions of their teams by asking the team's leadership to complete the worksheet.

If you are doing this work at the product level, with the example of our squad, we would ask Carlos (engineering architect), Jiang (lead developer), Jeffrey (senior designer), Jo (lead designer), Arun (designer), and Mei (product owner) to complete worksheets. Once the worksheets have converged into the future impact article for the software product, we would be sure to get the approval of the executive-level team.

1. Consider the level at which your vision is being established. Each leader at that level will complete the worksheet.

2. Choose the subject for your business impact worksheet (organization, product, service, etc.).

3. To develop a vision, completed worksheets should be merged into one vision as a future impact article that takes into consideration the contributions and expectations of each leader. (See that exercise for details.)

4. To gauge alignment or mine for disruptions, collect responses in a place available to all, and facilitate a team discussion around alignment or disruptions.

- Alignment: Are people seeing impact at significantly different levels (some very practical, others more visionary)? Have people discuss the different levels with the goal of aligning on what would be best for the customers and the business.

- Disruptions: Examine the possible disruptions based on their categories (customer, industry, business, team). Think about what would be most valuable to customers and the business.

5 If you are not working with a facilitator, identify a point person to collect the completed worksheets. Also identify who will be responsible for driving the next step, whether that be gaining alignment, identifying disruptions, or driving a vision. To be clear, this is a leadership role, not an administrative role. If someone is driving a vision, they should be able to *impartially* merge ideas into a future impact article.

6 Identify the names and roles of those who must complete the worksheet, as well as those who will approve the outcomes of whatever your next steps are.

7 Complete the current statement (see the example for instructions).

When you are ready, send out the worksheet to participants. I usually limit this to eight or ten people. The more participants you have, the longer it takes to synthesize the worksheets.

Understand Alignment and Mine for Disruptions
When using this exercise to see where teams are aligned or misaligned, or to mine for disruptions, simply note everyone's

ideas on either stickies or in collaboration software. Group similar ideas together, and keep outliers or specifically disruptive ideas separate. Then discuss:

- What are the implications of the outliers?
- Are there any that the team wants to take off the table?
- Are there any ideas that are particularly compelling?
- What ideas seem especially competitive, and what ideas would help you simply reach parity?

Note that we're not assuming that "alignment" is the same as "correct." We are using all this information to facilitate conversation. You may converge on the same statement, or you may be compelled to adjust it, based on an amazing idea that, through this exercise, is now seeing the light of day.

Crafting a Vision
If you are crafting or updating a vision, you will use the future impact article as the outcome of your synthesis of patterns and ideas. As the worksheets start to roll back in, get a jump-start on patterns by documenting them.

Example of Business Impact Worksheet
In this example, we will look at what the business impact worksheet might have looked like for a few of the people in our software squad—Jeffrey, Carlos, and Mei. In reality, the rest of the squad would have also completed the business impact worksheet, but three is enough for you to see the slightly different points of view. Of course, these are not real; I did my best to imagine myself as the different personas to illustrate that different roles see things differently. Read through the

three answers from the squad and note the differences. In the future impact article, I synthesize the three points of view.

Before you jump in, I want to draw your attention to the starting point. You need to start from somewhere. Here are some suggestions:

- A reasonable outcomes statement. Imperfect is fine, as this exercise either validates it or shows you where it might be elevated. (This is what I'll be using for the example.)
- An executive directional statement like "Always Home Mobile App, 2.0, powered by AI." It's something to get everyone thinking with plenty of room for imagining.
- An existing vision statement so you can validate, elevate, or update.

Instructions

- Read the current statement.
- Imagine that your team has made that statement come true, and it's six to twelve months later. With that frame of reference, complete the worksheet.

Business Impact Worksheet Template

Current Statement

[Write your current statement here]

Customer Impact

- What will customers be able to do in a year that they can't do today?
- What will customers no longer need to do?
- What five words would the customer use to describe their experience?
- What new people will be served?
- Are there any people that will no longer be served?

Market Impact

- What companies have been displaced by this work?
- What parts of the market do we own and why?
- Who is copying us and why?

Company or Organizational Impact
(Company, if this is C-suite; organizational, if below C-suite)

- How have we changed the way we work to achieve this success?
- What are the cultural keys to our success?

Software Squad Worksheet Example: Jeffrey, senior designer

Current Statement

Always Home will provide customers ages twenty-five to thirty-five with personalized recommendations of hotel amenities, local restaurants, and events so that they have a more convenient, enriched experience, a more delightful stay, and feel Always Home Hotels understands them.

Customer Impact

What will customers be able to do in a year that they can't do today?
- Have integration from any other app (e.g., Spotify, TIDAL, Ticketmaster, theme parks, autism-friendly events and locations) to book rooms at Always Home
- Integration with Instacart to have supplies and snacks in the room upon arrival for children
- Automatic, free laundry service for hotel members
- App will know kids and ages, and suggest cribs, kid beds, adjoining rooms
- Coordinate travel with friends and family through an online vacation plan

What will customers no longer need to do?
- Bounce between apps to figure out their vacation; less coordination with family and friends
- Pack so much

What five words would the customer use to describe their experience?
- Convenient
- Fun
- Easy
- Happy kids

What new people will be served?
- Taking back the demographic of twenty-five to thirty-five

Are there any people that will no longer be served?
- Nope, keeping our existing customers

Market Impact

What companies have been displaced by this work?
- None. We took back demographic from Airbnb, but it won't be displaced, due to the breadth of its business.

What parts of the market do we own and why?
- Young parents because Airbnb gives this demographic control, but we cater to them.

Who is copying us and why?
- All our competitors because we are winning this demographic.

Company or Organizational Impact
(Company, if this is C-suite; organizational, if below C-suite)

How have we changed the way we work to achieve this success?
- We've rallied around this demographic in a way we never did before. The problems we were solving were very human problems, not technical ones.
- We incorporated people from this target demographic into our product lifecycle to make sure we hit their targets—we were really led by the customer.
- We worked with other areas in ways we never did before, such as hotel operations (to bring deliveries to rooms, etc.) for a total end-to-end experience.

What are the cultural keys to our success?
- Valuing the customer's needs and experience above our own opinions
- Building our success on the customer's success
- Radical collaboration—we mostly did away with silos
- Psychological safety
- Be ready to let go of our ideas if they don't help the customer

Software Squad Worksheet Example: Carlos, architect

Current Statement

Always Home will provide customers ages twenty-five to thirty-five with personalized recommendations of hotel amenities, local restaurants, and events so that they have a more convenient, enriched experience, a more delightful stay, and feel Always Home Hotels understands them.

Customer Impact

What will customers be able to do in a year that they can't do today?
- Have app integration with event recommendations, driven by AI
- Have rooms prepared for kids
- Coordinate travel with friends and family

What will customers no longer need to do?
- Bounce between apps and websites
- Pack as much stuff
- Worry about the needs of their children

What five words would the customer use to describe their experience?
- The
- Kids
- Are
- Not
- Fussing

What new people will be served?
- Twenty-five- to thirty-five-year-olds with families

Are there any people that will no longer be served?
- n/a

Market Impact

What companies have been displaced by this work?
- n/a

What parts of the market do we own and why?
- Young families

Who is copying us and why?
- All our competitors, for sure, because we disrupted the concept of hospitality. And maybe some other entertainment or hospitality companies will seek us out to partner.

Company or Organizational Impact
(Company, if this is C-suite; organizational, if below C-suite)

How have we changed the way we work to achieve this success?
- Engineering is part of customer feedback sessions.
- We have deep integration across features throughout the Always Home mobile application, the Always Home website, and our new entertainment and hospitality partners.
- We have constant streams of new data coming in that enhance our ability to know, understand, and predict our customers' changing needs (e.g., as their kids age, new ones come along).

What are the cultural keys to our success?
- Collaboration
- Customer-first
- Alignment before we act

Software Squad Worksheet Example: Mei, product owner

Current Statement

Always Home will provide customers ages twenty-five to thirty-five with personalized recommendations of hotel amenities, local restaurants, and events so that they have a more convenient, enriched experience, a more delightful stay, and feel Always Home Hotels understands them.

Customer Impact

What will customers be able to do in a year that they can't do today?
- With the new integrations provided across multiple entertainment applications, along with AI recommendations and personalization, customers will be able to organize and schedule a kid-friendly vacation in under fifteen minutes.
- Families will have the conveniences that they need when traveling with kids, including food, OTC medicines, diapers and supplies, free same-day laundry service, maid service scheduled at their convenience, toys and games, and water wings and pool toys.

What will customers no longer need to do?
- Navigate through multiple apps and websites over the course of days to match event dates to hotel availability
- Pack as much stuff
- Worry about their kids
- Deal with cranky kids once they get to the hotel

What five words would the customer use to describe their experience?
- Actually restful!
- Let's do it again! (That's six—sorry!)

What new people will be served?
- Taking back the demographic of twenty-five to thirty-five

Are there any people that will no longer be served?
- n/a

Market Impact
What companies have been displaced by this work? • n/a—making an opportunity out of a gap
What parts of the market do we own and why? • Young parents, and a new demographic—kids! If we do this right, they will ask for Always Home vacations because they're so fun.
Who is copying us and why? • All our competitors because we shined a light on the gap—we need to stay vigilant!
Company or Organizational Impact (Company, if this is C-suite; organizational, if below C-suite)
How have we changed the way we work to achieve this success? • We all understand the customer and see that kids are our customers too. • We work much more closely with the customer throughout all our collaboration sessions and testing. • We are considering non-hotel companies as partners, which opens a lot of doors for us.
What are the cultural keys to our success? • Building our success on the customer's success • Radical collaboration • Psychological safety

Exercise 7: Future Impact Article

What It Is
In this exercise, you converge the answers from the business impact worksheets into a single story, resembling an article in your favorite industry publication. The goal is to pull together all the points of view into a vision that any reader will be able to see, understand, and get behind. You are taking what may feel like a list of features or a statement that still seems a little abstract and fleshing it out for all involved: users, competition, and your business. Using the form of an article encourages you to look for the cause and effect between the sections.

When to Use It
In conjunction with the business impact worksheet.

How to Do It
You take a journalist's point of view and use the business impact information to talk about all the great impacts this vision, product release, service, or what have you has had on the customers and market, as well as how the company got the job done.

Here is a helpful order of operations:

1 Document patterns and outliers for each section of questions. This helps you organize information so you can move faster.

2 Put on your creativity hat and start telling a story! Your goal is to get people to see possibilities and opportunities. It can be helpful to review a few articles and grab some choice words or phrases to help you along.

3   As you write, keep it light. Touch on a concept, then talk about its impact.

4   A good length is 600 to 800 words.

Once the future impact article is complete, send it out for review. Then gather people back together to discuss what they liked and might want to move forward on. You are working from a So That statement, so you can update it and any cascading with the team. Or you can swizzle the future impact article into a vision statement.

As you read, you will see I embellished as new ideas came to me. Do that! Make the article pop off the page and into the imaginations of the readers. You want readers to feel inspired and excited to act. Of course, this isn't an exact blueprint of your vision, but it will spark conversation.

Home Never Felt So Good! Always Home Cements Itself as an Industry Leader in Modern Customer Experiences
By Sarah Plantenberg

START WITH A PROBLEM SETUP anchored by a real quote from an executive For a decade, the hospitality industry has been trying to find its way through the disruption of Airbnb, Vrbo, and other platforms that put vacationers in touch with renters. The hotel industry has been especially plagued by this situation, with the old guard, like Always Home Hotels, taking the hardest hits. Carol Johnson, vice president of Software, said of the problem, "It's entirely our responsibility to stay in touch with our users, and we failed. But we learned our lesson, let me tell you, and that won't happen again!"

THE NEXT SECTION gives the reader a summary of the overall impact and imagines a way to substantiate that with some data. Always Home boasts a more delightful stay, full of conveniences to enrich the experience of families in particular, and they have the data to prove it. A survey of 137 recent young family guests revealed that 87 percent would definitely use Always Home's new AI-powered application to organize and book their next vacation, with 95 percent of those respondents saying that they could tell Always Home understood them by the services they provided. In an effort to build relationships with these families that will last for generations, Always Home actually surveyed the child guests! Anyone aged four and up staying at the hotel got an Always Home plush toy hotel for answering three questions: 1) Did you like the snacks? 2) What other snacks should we buy? and 3) Did you get to use any of the pool toys? (Of course, kids under three got a plush toy too.)

NOW WE GIVE the reader some specifics so they can visualize what the customer experience could look like. While Always Home's competitors have been targeting amenities for adults, such as restaurants with top chefs and credits to nearby casinos, Always Home focused on the whole family. Through competitive and user research, Always Home saw that Airbnb was a great choice for providing families with more control, but with that control came work. Always Home took that work into their own hands, creating a new kind of hotel experience for families. Using their mobile application, which seamlessly integrates with almost a dozen other entertainment and hospitality apps, Always Home can read your calendar, the availability of tickets, and its own free days to recommend a perfectly balanced vacation *and* leisure for all. All you need to do is opt in through the mobile app, and Always Home does the rest. Their goal was for a family of four to book a vacation (airline integration coming soon!) in fifteen minutes or less—and they did it!

THIS SECTION TALKS ABOUT changes that need to happen in the organization and inspires the reader to see the value of change. How did Always Home, one of the seniors on the block, come up with such a comprehensive, competitive idea? "Radical collaboration is the name of the game," said Carlos Fuentes, the technical architect in charge of bringing this concept to life. Teaming together, the product owners, designers, and technical staff wrote a contract that spelled out what they wanted their culture to be like, as well as their goals: agility, nimbleness, customer-centric, and collaborative. They focused on building the foundations of trust and psychological safety so that any idea, no matter how off-the-wall it seemed, was welcome and considered. In this fertile soil, the seeds of creativity were planted. This is how the team realized that if the kids were happy, the parents would be happy, and the focus shifted to include the next generation of hotel guests.

HERE WE HAVE the impact on the market. How is the hospitality market reacting? Well, hotels are back on the map for families with small children—at least Always Home is. Others in the old guard appear to be scrambling to keep up. Where Always Home integrated with Instacart to have products for children of all ages in the room before guests arrived, other traditional hotels seemed to have missed the mark. A small gift basket of nuts and fruit are not the same to a three-year-old as Lunchables, or microwave mac and cheese might be to a fifteen-year-old. The bar is set even higher with Always Home giving up the efficiency of controlling their housekeeping staff's schedule, so that families can book the service according to their own needs, rather than dodging out of the room by 10 a.m.

CLOSE with a punchy summary. Suffice it to say that Always Home's market share of young families is rising fast, as are their revenues and stock price. And it's well deserved. The thoughtfulness with which Always Home addresses its customers' needs is the response we've been waiting for from the hotel industry. Dare we say that Always Home is shaking up Airbnb? I think we do.

Exercise 8: Team Purpose

What It Is

This is one of the richest exercises in the book. We do this exercise so that:

- Everyone understands how the different disciplines or roles—and the individuals in those disciplines or roles—fit together to make a functioning system.
- People see how the system serves the organizational mission.
- People find synergies that can be leveraged.
- People see where friction can be reduced by addressing overlaps and divergence.

The purpose exercise also draws out the "why" for each participating discipline that works together and offers opportunities to see how you can work together better. In this exercise, each discipline in the team or organization will learn what the others contribute *from the vantage points of the members of the contributing disciplines*. This vantage point is critical; it's why this exercise is so successful. Team members discover assumptions they make about one another's needs, thoughts, interests, and more. Where these assumptions are wrong, they can be corrected.

People also learn if they have underestimated each other's talents and contributions, which can happen simply out of ignorance. Up-leveling everyone's understanding of each other's talents and potential contributions up-levels the entire team by showing everyone what *could* be if they made a few changes. Along these same lines, teams sometimes find areas of synergy—places where they could work together for more impact. You will also mine for gaps that need to be closed and overlaps that are causing different kinds of friction.

As people understand their own and each other's professional identities, this exercise also reveals insights about individual and team motivation.

When to Use It

Use this exercise:

- When a cross-functional team needs to better understand itself and how it works

- When a team or organization is struggling with operational inefficiencies or working with other teams

- At intersection points between teams or when adding a new discipline to an existing process to identify the most efficient, cost-effective handoffs between the teams that will drive the best outcomes

- When reorganizing to make sure you craft your organizations with the amplification of talent in mind

How to Do It

1. Break out into groups composed of roles or disciplines.
   - Each discipline should use a different colored sticky, shape, or some other indicator if using a spreadsheet or document. As you group your answers, you will need to differentiate between disciplines.

2. Have each individual answer the questions on the template. They should do so as if speaking for the whole team, not simply themselves.
   - Why does our team exist?
   - Why are we good at what we do?
   - What do people say about us?
   - What are we great at?

3. Share answers among those within your discipline and converge the responses to get to no more than three answers per question. Each answer will be written on a single sticky. Rewrite, rephrase—do whatever you need to do to combine and synthesize so that everyone feels the answers best represent the team. Choose someone to read out the answers on behalf of the team.

4. Read out answers following the method described in The Flow section, grouping and labeling as you go.

5. Mine for synergies, overlaps, divergences, and gaps, as described in The Flow, noting everything as you go and assigning owners.

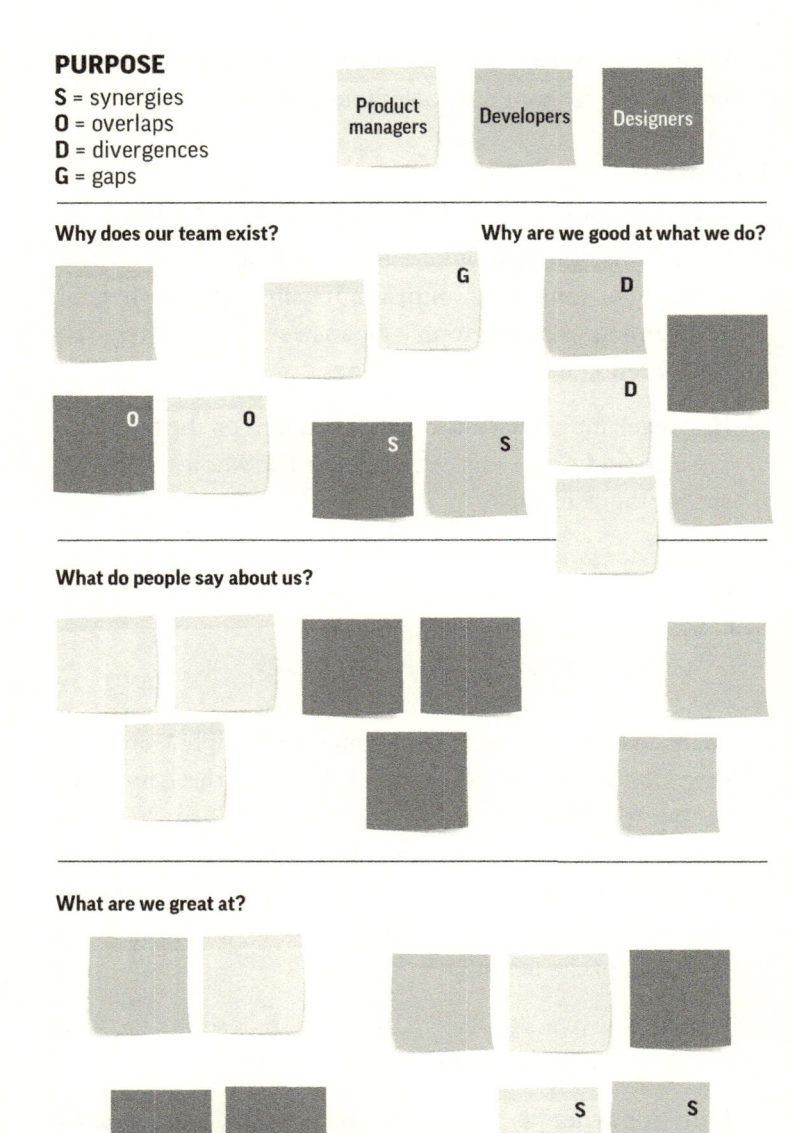

PURPOSE
S = synergies
O = overlaps
D = divergences
G = gaps

Product managers | Developers | Designers

Why does our team exist? **Why are we good at what we do?**

G

D

D

O   O

S   S

What do people say about us?

What are we great at?

S   S

The most important thing people can do during this readout is to actively listen to understand what each discipline does from the standpoint of the experts. Listen to understand how your colleagues see their purpose, so that you can adjust your perspective.

Exercise 9: People Vision

What It Is

In this exercise, the team will illustrate what the ideal organization should look, feel, and sound like so that you share a common vision for success, imagine the ideal culture in action, and discern the values that motivate people's choices. You also want to see and understand any differences between people's answers. Everyone does this exercise individually, imagining they work in the perfect environment. They then converge answers to form an ideal environment for everyone. Will you actually get the perfect environment? Maybe not. But maybe you will! You certainly will get closer than if you didn't do this work.

Here, as we've talked about so often in *Driving Outcomes*, you will make the implicit explicit. Creating clear targets, which everyone can imagine, clarifies what existing norms ought to be abandoned, which can stay, and what new norms need to be put into place to create the right conditions for success. Looking at the ideal organization from all angles, and through the eyes of each participant, helps everyone to be very clear, and it leaves little room for interpretation.

When to Use It

If you haven't intentionally designed your culture and identified how that translates into behavioral norms and daily operations, you should do this exercise. You will almost certainly find ways to reduce or eliminate friction points. This exercise is also great to do:

- Any time teams change
- Any time processes change
- When new leadership joins a team or organization
- When there is a change to vision, or any major change to a team or organization
- At regular intervals (e.g., every six months or annually) to keep your culture in tip-top shape

These questions are also interesting to discuss during job interviews with prospective employees.

How to Do It

1 Individuals privately answer the following questions. People may have more than one answer per question. There may not be enough time for everyone to share every answer so practice your prioritization. The numbering in these templates will seem out of order. Complete them in numerical order, even though it requires you to move back and forth between templates to complete this exercise.

- Each discipline should use a different colored sticky, shape, or some other indicator if using a spreadsheet or document. As you group your answers, you will need to differentiate between disciplines.

Question 1: In a perfect world, describe what the team would look and act like when you are all working synergistically together.
- What behaviors do you see?
- What kinds of communication styles do you see?
- How is conflict handled?
- How are successes handled?
- What happens when someone has a new idea that might disrupt the current flow?
- What processes, communications, or other things stop happening?

Question 2: In a perfect world, success feels like...
- Describe what it feels like to be a member of this team.
- What does it feel like to know your team trusts you and that you can trust your team?
- What does it feel like to make a mistake or to not have the answer?
- How do you want your team members to feel when they make a mistake or misunderstand something?
- How do you want your team members to feel when they have a great idea?

Question 3: Success does *not* look like...
- List the top three thoughts that come to mind.

Question 4: Success does *not* feel like...
- List the top three thoughts that come to mind.

1. In a perfect world, what does the team look and act like?

Behaviors

Communication styles

When in conflict or disrupted

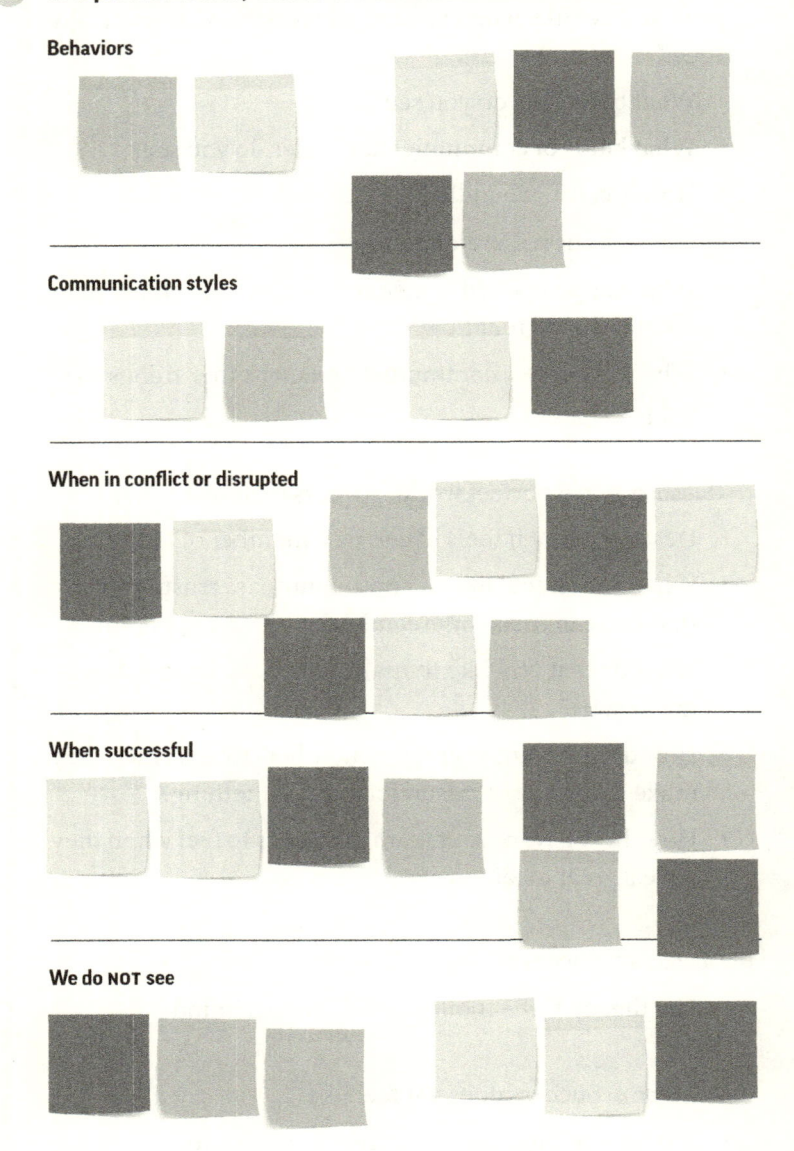

When successful

We do NOT see

2. In a perfect world, what would it feel like...

To be a member of this team?

To know your team trusts you and that you can trust your team?

To make a mistake or not have the answer?

(3) What success does NOT look like

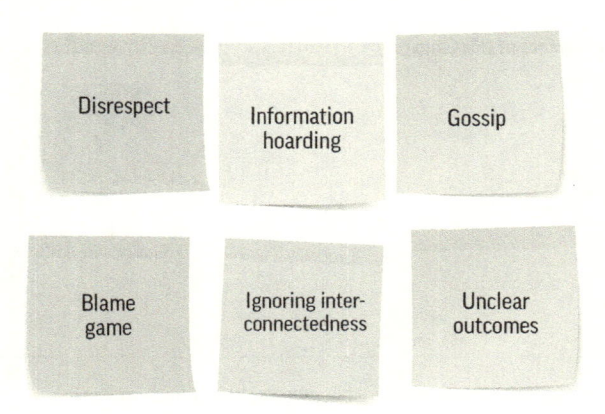

- Disrespect
- Information hoarding
- Gossip
- Blame game
- Ignoring interconnectedness
- Unclear outcomes

2. Share your answers using the method in The Flow.

3. Reflect on the clusters and outliers, then discuss. The goal is to understand what the ideal state looks like and to see yourselves there. You are not yet solving for differences. For example, some people might say that conflict is handled in a transparent manner within the team, and others might say conflict is handled privately. You're not actually going to resolve this difference right now. You're doing this work to understand what behaviors and choices you want your values to drive. For this example, conflict might be handled by placing value on the needs of everyone, which would imply that conflict is handled in a way that best suits that individual. That would then be written into the contract. At this point, simply note differences, but don't worry about them just yet.

Move on to the values exercise to get clear on what underlying values must be present for this vision to take place.

4 **What success does NOT feel like**

- Scary
- Threatening
- Going solo
- Protecting myself
- Hiding info

Exercise 10: Values

What It Is

In Chapter 2, I defined culture as the expression of what an organization truly values. If you're doing these exercises in order, you will have described what your culture looks like using the people vision exercise. Now you will converge on the values visible in that expression of your optimal people vision. You are reverse engineering your culture to find what drives the behavioral norms that will make your optimal people vision possible. We do this so that every member of the team is clear on what is important, and so that every member can use the same values as guides for making judgments in their day-to-day work.

When to Use It

Use this exercise after you have gone through the people vision exercise.

How to Do It

1 Each individual reflects on the clusters in the people vision and comes up with five or six values they see reflected, which they feel are critical to the success of the team. Here are some examples to jump-start your team, but please add your own:

- Accountability
- Adaptability
- Alignment
- Collaboration
- Commitment to great outcomes
- Continuous improvement
- Growth
- Innovation
- Psychological safety
- Responsibility
- Responsiveness
- Transparency in all things
- Trust

2 Read out the answers exactly as you did in the people vision exercise, clustering and labeling clusters as you go.

3 Discuss both the clusters and the outliers among the team. Nest values within other values, if that makes sense, or draw connectors. For example, I believe psychological safety assumes trust and accountability. You may end up with quite a web, or you may end up simplifying to the

highest-level values. Do whatever best reflects for the team which values should be driving their choices.

4. Define anti-patterns to remove any ambiguity. Go through the list of top-level values the team has agreed upon, and as a group, agree on the opposite value—this is just a thought experiment. (See contrarian thinking for more information on this approach.) This might bring up some interesting conversations or opportunities for clarification. For example, if the team values responsibility, the anti-pattern to that is irresponsibility. What does that mean? How do you know when you are being irresponsible? The team may need to nest a few other values underneath like responsiveness, communication, and transparency. If it doesn't bring anything up, great; you've spent a short amount of time confirming that everyone understands the values. If it does bring something up, work through it until everyone understands.

5. Check the values the team has decided on against your people vision. Is there anything left unaddressed? Any potential ambiguity in what needs to be valued for success to be achieved? Anything that is valued that looks like it could interrupt success? Reconcile these areas by shifting the values, redefining success, or both.

6. Make values transparent. This will be an action item for later, but get the following written down with owners:

   - Everyone gets a copy of the values.

   - Add reading the values out loud to agendas for at least two regular meetings each week. These can be daily scrums, weekly staff meetings, retrospectives, whenever you gather. Doing this will start helping you build new habits.

Exercise 11: Contract for Change

What It Is

The contract for change documents changes in behavioral norms. These changes are pulled directly from the workshop and reflect what the team needs to do to achieve the business outcomes. Everyone should have a copy of the contract visible in their workspace. To help build new habits, read it out loud in staff meetings to remind people of the changes to which they have committed. If you have not done the workshop yet, you can experiment with the contract for change by imagining outcomes you would like for your team.

When to Use It

After the team has workshopped, use it to document what behavioral norms will be the focus of the next quarter to drive outcomes.

You can also use it as an individual (doer or leader) as a thought experiment to ignite conversations around the alignment of outcomes and culture.

How to Do It

Moving from left to right, write down what the team should start doing and stop doing to achieve the outcome. This can be a great topic of discussion for a team or for a team to bring to their leadership to spark change.

Whether doing a contract for change as a thought experiment or in a workshop, you may have more than one answer in the By Doing and And by *Not* Doing columns for a single outcome. If that happens and the changes are too much to do at one time, you can prioritize a few to start with. Revisit the contract for change every few weeks to tick off the items you've accomplished and then address the next priorities. It is recommended that teams work on four or five outcomes at a time, and revisit them quarterly.

Contract for Change

Team Outcome	By Doing	And by *Not* Doing

Contract for Change Example

Team Outcome	By Doing	And by *Not* Doing
Protect creative time for the design team so they have more time to innovate	Blocking off calendars Wednesday and Friday from 2 to 5 p.m.	Booking the team with more work than will fit into a 34-hour week
Make culture a priority to reduce friction and improve employee engagement, performance, and business outcomes	Holding weekly retrospectives Scheduling quarterly culture and contract reviews Taking action on all open items Holding ourselves and each other accountable	Staying silent in the face of discomfort
Improve psychological safety in team meetings to reduce friction	Arriving to meetings on time Repeating the speaker's point and making sure you understand before responding to the point Using "I statements" Assuming the best motivation Checking self-awareness before meetings	Assuming intent Interrupting/ talking over Allowing emotions to run over
Facilitate alignment to reduce friction and improve operations	Leaders ensuring that vision and purpose are clear Measuring what matters	Leaving it to teams to decipher what the vision is or when success has been reached

Exercise 12: Doable Versus Valuable

What It Is

This is an alignment exercise to reduce the potential for friction throughout your organization. It is one of the most valuable exercises I've used. I wish I had invented it, but it's part of the standard design thinking toolkit.

This activity helps you figure out where to place your investment. As the name suggests, you weigh the value provided to the user versus the level of investment required to do the thing. This technique aligns everyone around where investments should be made and why, and it removes a lot of potential for cognitive and psychological friction.

Let's say Mei (the product owner) wants to include a feature in the hotel's mobile application that will cost a lot of development time and be very expensive to build. Ethan (CTO) hears about it and shoots it down. He's not going to blow a quarter's worth of development budget on one feature. Welcome, psychological friction, Mei's been waiting for you! These kinds of conversations can feel like a tug-of-war because they're difficult to have. But this doable versus valuable exercise will help Ethan verbalize his thoughts on making an investment, while still taking the context of Mei's goals into consideration and vice versa. They examine the totality of the consequences of doing one thing versus another, rather than ping-ponging between value for Mei and cost for Ethan. You can change the titles of the two axes to be any two things that are in conflict with one another. You may find that the two things are not in conflict; the business model underneath is in conflict. This tool will help you have the right conversation.

Strategic moves or decisions about what to build should be guided by a business outcome, and then you can budget accordingly. After all, that's what the money is for.

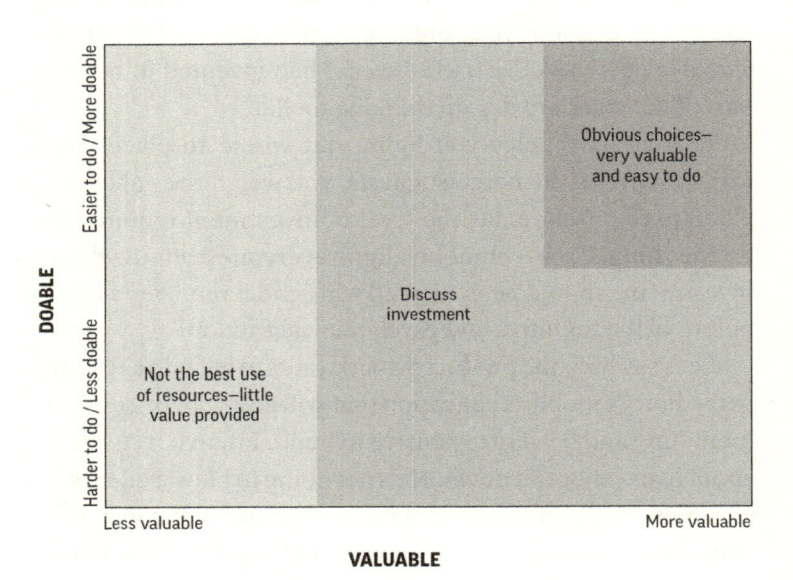

DOABLE (y-axis: Harder to do / Less doable → Easier to do / More doable)
VALUABLE (x-axis: Less valuable → More valuable)

- Obvious choices—very valuable and easy to do
- Discuss investment
- Not the best use of resources—little value provided

When to Use It

Use this exercise:

- When you cannot decide if what you are building is worth the investment
- To narrow down a group of ideas (from your business impact worksheet or any ideation that needs narrowing down), while also having a sense of what your budget can tolerate

- When people are motivated by two different business paradigms, like Mei (value to the user) and Ethan (funding development for multiple features)

How to Do It

1 Write all the ideas under debate on stickies.

2 Have everyone vote on both the do-ability of each idea and the value to the user. Everyone gets five votes for each category and can spend them in any way they like. In other words, for the five doable votes, you can vote on five different things, split your votes across few different ideas, or cast all five votes on one thing (each person must cast all votes). The more votes you post on one idea, the more doable you think it is. Then repeat the voting process for value to the user.

3 Tally up the total votes for each category and write it on the sticky. For example, if Idea A got a total of seven doable votes and four value votes, write on a corner of the sticky "D=7 / V=4."

4 Now plot these ideas on the template according to the number of votes for each category. Your Y axis is doable for the team, and your X axis is value for the user.

5 Step back and discuss. Where things land on the template is not the final answer; it's a visualization tool to help you have a thoughtful discussion about how your investment should impact your business outcomes. This exercise is designed to help you evaluate choices and weigh consequences. The number of votes is not meant to be the deciding factor; votes simply tell you where people are at the moment.

Example: Team of 6 people voting; each person has 5 votes

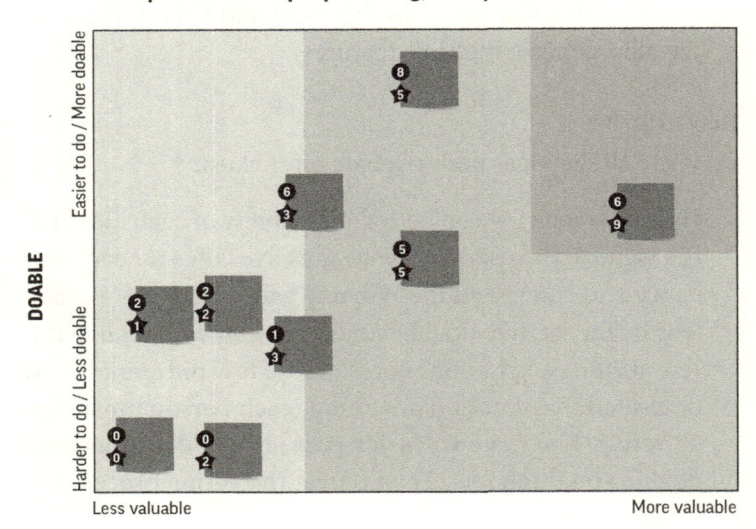

- Doable
- ★ Valuable

Exercise 13: Contrarian Thinking

What It Is

A contrarian is someone who takes the opposite point of view or attitude. In this exercise, you practice challenging your own thoughts by experimenting with their opposites. This exercise can be done with other people as well. The goal is to find clarity.

For example, if you are unsure of a solution or a direction, examine the opposite solution or direction to discover boundaries, edges, and different ways of looking at things. I do this, and suggest this to designers, when we are unclear about what should go onto the virtual page. Our contrarian approach would be something like designing the absolute worst interaction we could possibly imagine for the user. You'll be surprised at how well this helps you home in on the areas of critical function. For inspiration, check out the series called "The Uncomfortable" by Katerina Kamprani, which you can find online. Her work is an examination of function and purpose, and she is absolutely brilliant.

Contrarian thinking functions in a number of ways.

- It helps you find boundaries amid ambiguity. You can't always see the boundaries from the inside. Sometimes you need to step outside and walk around to get the full picture.

- It is highly useful for the creation of contracts for change. Write down the new desired behavior and its opposite. This helps to get everyone clear on what not to do. The boundaries may not always be clear to everyone.

- It reveals important considerations that were not on your radar.

- It opens up creativity, especially when the contrarian thoughts reach levels of absurdity. Once you get going, this work can lead teams into hysterical laughter. Laughing regulates the nervous system, telling the brain it's safe to relax and feel vulnerable. There's a lot of research documenting the role of play in innovation. Make a game out of it and have fun.

When to Use It

Use contrarian thinking whenever you are stuck or unsure which direction to go next. Pick an option and then take it to the opposite extreme, and repeat. I guarantee it will help you gravitate toward some specific options while eliminating others.

Stuck with a problem statement and don't know how to get started with the solution? Rewrite the problem statement as its opposite and see what doors that opens.

Unsure if your solution really solves the problem? Consider the opposite solution and see what you learn about the nuances of both the problem and the solution.

Once you feel you're done with a body of work, validate it by considering the opposite of the key points.

Exercise 14: Ideation

What It Is

Ideation is simply the technique of generating and developing ideas. In Chapter 8, we talked about a method for embracing constraints. I recommend using ideation as an innovation technique to brainstorm your way around obstacles.

When to Use It

When you run into constraints or obstacles, take a few minutes to throw some new ideas on the table. Fresh ideas break up the logjam of traditional thought that has you backed into a corner.

How to Do It

You can do this alone, but I recommend pulling together a team of un-like-minded people. Yes, differently thinking people generate a kaleidoscope of ideas that play off each other.

- State your problem clearly in a place where everyone can see it (for example, on a whiteboard).

- Set a timer for ten or fifteen minutes. While the timer is counting down, everyone writes ideas on stickies that move the needle on the problem. These don't need to be complete solutions but big ideas. Two or three ideas need to be wild, outlandish ideas that could never actually be done. This adds a level of absurdity to the ideation. Since everyone will be putting down absurd ideas, people feel freer to challenge their own preconceived notions and push the boundaries. These ideas can quickly open the door to new ways of thinking. One idea per sticky.

- When time is up, go around the room and share your ideas with each other.

- Collect similar ideas together and give them a useful label. Collect all the outlier ideas together, those that are especially innovative, so you don't lose them.

- Discuss how ideation has changed your perception of the problem. Do you understand it the same way? Do you have any novel ideas for getting around the problem?

Acknowledgments

MY FRIENDS AND FAMILY, especially:

Joani Albano and Andi Plantenberg, there is no better support system in the world. I am truly blessed to be one leaf of this clover. I love you.

Barbara Stender and Gretchen Plantenberg, the best cheering section a person could have. I soar on your energy and enthusiasm.

Marge Chiuminatto and John Plantenberg for your encouragement and support.

David Levinson for your friendship and support throughout this process, and for being such an excellent design partner in crime for so many years. You've challenged me and made me a better designer, manager, and person.

Molly Bigelow for your continued support. It has been such a pleasure to know you and work with you. You are simply brilliant.

Esther Kim for your faith and encouragement from the moment we met and especially as I journeyed into authorship.

Peggy, my love, for your comfort and unconditional love.

I'd like to acknowledge the editing and publishing support I've received, especially:

Brooke White, editor par excellence. Thank you for helping me find my voice and reach new levels of authenticity. Also, everyone at Page Two for their excellent care and guidance. What a gift to work with you all and to be counted in your community of authors.

Peter Economy, you are a kind, generous editor and coach. Thank you very much for helping me understand what I was getting into and helping me actually get into it!

For those who helped me jump-start this effort, especially:

Rob Purdy for helping me gain momentum. I can't wait to read *your* book when the time comes. I hope we can work together again, soon.

Jim Patton for your thoughts, advice, and generosity.

All the clients with whom I've had the privilege of working for the last twenty-five years. This book is for you.

About the Author

SARAH PLANTENBERG is an expert in the field of human factors who has worked at the intersection of human beings, technology, and business for more than twenty-five years. She has been in the roles of software designer, business designer, strategist, and innovator of technology and methodology. As co-founder of the IBM Garage, a lean cloud adoption consultancy, and its companion methodology, IBM Garage Methodology, Sarah has helped springboard hundreds of organizations into their digital transformation journey.

Sarah brings together disparate points of view across even the most complex teams, teaching them to align on business outcomes, as well as design and maintain the culture needed to drive to those outcomes. Sarah is an avid inventor, and she holds nine technical and user experience patents through her employers.

Find her on LinkedIn at linkedin.com/in/sarah-plantenberg or visit her website at driving-outcomes.com.

Five Ways to Accelerate Your Change

1. **Team Workshops:** Teamwork is the key to reducing friction at scale. Let me help you coordinate your team into a nimble, responsive school of fish! The workshop uses the exercises in this book, along with others designed specifically for teams at the intersection of different disciplines, to define outcomes, values, and ultimately design the culture that will drive your business outcomes.

2. **Facilitation Training:** Bring *Driving Outcomes* facilitation skills in-house with our facilitator training! This will help you keep your momentum and scale your culture across other teams or business units. This is an excellent option for organizations that intend to keep their culture current by becoming responsive to the forces that pressure their business.

3. **Leadership Coaching for Executives and Leaders:** Gain leadership skills specifically designed to support your teams as they design and maintain a culture that drives your specific business outcomes. We can do this through one-on-one coaching, as a coordinated effort across multiple levels of leadership, or a combination of the two.

4. **Speaking at Events:** Are there people in your organization contributing to a poor culture? Or maybe you want to drive deeper engagement by reinvigorating and inspiring your team? Let me open the door for you to the larger conversation about the relationship between culture and outcomes, the invisible maze that introduces friction, and what you can do about it.

5. **Copies for Your Organization:** Buy copies of *Driving Outcomes* for your organization. Contact me for special offers and bulk discounts.

Reach out to discuss these options or the unique needs of your organization. I can't wait to work together.

Made in the USA
Las Vegas, NV
01 March 2025

18911898R00163